Thirteen Going on Twenty

PENNEY SCHWAB

BETHANY HOUSE PUBLISHERS

MINNEAPOLIS, MINNESOTA 55438

A Division of Bethany Fellowship, Inc.

Portions of this material originally appeared in *MARRIAGE and Family Living* magazine, March 1982.

Published by Bethany House Publishers
A Division of Bethany Fellowship, Inc.
6820 Auto Club Road, Minneapolis, MN 55438

Printed in the United States of America

Library of Congress Cataloging in Publication Data

Schwab, Penney, 1943-
   Thirteen going on twenty.

   1. Youth—United States. 2. Adolescent psychology—United States. 3. Parent and child—United States. 4. Parenting—United States—Religious aspects—Christianity. I. Title.
HQ769.S4185   1983   305.2'35'0973   83-12292
ISBN 0-87123-587-0

For my three, plus one:
Patrick, Michael,
Rebecca, and
Sarah

The Author

PENNY V. SCHWAB is a freelance writer from Copeland, Kansas. She attended Oklahoma State University and took a course in professional writing from the University of Oklahoma. She and her husband, Don, have 3 children ranging in age from 14 to 18.

Preface

When my children were toddlers, older parents often told me, "Just wait until those kids are teenagers. Then you'll find out what *real* trouble is!"

Well, I waited. My sons, Patrick and Michael, are now nineteen and eighteen. My daughter Rebecca is fifteen. Yes, there have been trials and troubles and heartaches. But these years haven't been the horror-filled time I was led to expect. Instead, I consider them a reward for all the days of wet diapers, sleepless nights, *Sesame Street* reruns, and shepherd costumes for church plays.

This book contains my prayers for our family—and for all teens and their parents. Even though the characters are fictitious, each incident is drawn from real life; many are things my own teenagers experienced, others happened to their friends and acquaintances. I hope many readers will benefit from our successes—and our mistakes. I pray that every parent of a teen will know the special joy that comes from living with children who are thirteen going on twenty.

Acknowledgments

Many people helped make this book possible, and I am grateful to all of them. My husband, Don, lent moral support plus a hand with the housework. My children and their friends freely offered thoughts and ideas. Mr. Daniel Gottry suggested and encouraged the project. Mrs. Carol Johnson and the editorial staff of Bethany House Publishers gave valuable tips for developing the manuscript. I owe special thanks to my good friends Glenda Patterson and Maria Hutley; their prayer and practical support never wavered.

Table of Contents

Introduction

The Beginning of the End

School started today, Lord. Lance and Laurie tried to act nonchalant, but they couldn't suppress the anticipation and excitement each new school year brings.

In a way, this year marks the beginning of the end—the end of our family as it's been for as long as I can remember. Lance will be eighteen soon, legally an adult. This is the last year he'll be a live-at-home part of our circle. Laurie is a sophomore. Sometimes she's fifteen going on twenty, at other times fifteen going back to twelve.

I think it's harder to be a teenager now than it used to be. Pressures are tremendous—pressures to individually do and be, to "make it big," and at the same time to totally conform. Drink and drugs are readily available. Cults actively recruit on many high school campuses. Sexual experiences are the norm for many teens. But even these are easier to resist than the everyday temptations—to cheat on a test, to lie and thus avoid trouble, to pass on that bit of gossip, and to surround oneself with a tight circle of friends and say "keep out" to the rest of the world.

Lord, my husband and I have tried to rear Laurie and Lance as *your* children. We've attended Sunday school and worship services as a family, and been active in the programs of our church. We've talked with them about you and what you expect of our lives. We've studied your Word and encouraged the children to do so.

Now, with our time together growing short, I am as-

11

sailed by doubts. I'm afraid I haven't done enough. I've let other concerns push you to the fringes of our home. I've been too harsh at times, too lenient at others. Worst of all, I haven't always been the example I should have been.

You have promised to hear me when I pray. Maybe that's what I'm called to do right now. I ask your blessing on Lance and Laurie. And I ask your blessing on their friends—on Beth, who is as dear to me as a daughter, and Kerri, Jason, and Mark; on the boys and girls they date; and the people who touch their lives. Make your presence real to them, Father; help them grow into the men and women you want them to be.

Thank you for these teenagers. Guide them, and me, throughout this all-important year.

1

Thirteen Going on Twenty

Who Am I?

"Why don't you write something for the magazines I read?" Laurie asked. "A story Beth and Kerri and I would like."

So I did. Only I kept it a secret. I told myself I wanted Laurie to be surprised when she opened her favorite magazine and saw my name. Deep down, though, I was afraid of her reaction. You see, the piece was entitled, "My Other Parents." Laurie, like the girl in the story, is an adopted child.

Laurie came to us when she was eight days old. Lance wanted to name her Cinderella, and was outraged when we didn't. We dressed her in a frilly white dress, a gift from a proud grandma. Her tiny legs stuck out like chicken bones, and her face was wreathed with a cloud of dark hair. We carried her in a green wicker basket during the five-hundred-mile drive to our home. She screamed for the next six months, and had terrible temper tantrums for five years.

From the instant we saw her, Laurie was part of our family. She is so much the child of my heart I sometimes forget that another mother's love gave her life, another mother's womb nourished her.

Seeing us together, people often say, "Laurie is your image!" Strictly speaking, it isn't true; Laurie is smaller, prettier, and has brilliant blue eyes instead of my brown ones. But we have the same color hair and facial bone structure. We're both poor at math but love to read. We both black out if we stand up too quickly, have second toes longer than our big ones, and are prone to circles under our eyes.

But being a chosen child, however much loved, isn't easy. "Who am I?", the question every teenager asks, assumes added significance when she literally does not know! Laurie has two other parents somewhere, and other grandparents. She may have brothers and sisters. It's only natural that she should wonder. Laurie believes, though, as we do, that long before her birth, God wanted her to be the child that made our family circle complete.

For that, dear Lord, I am deeply grateful. That belief has guided us through troubles that might otherwise have destroyed our mutual love. Please keep Laurie secure in the knowledge that she is ours, and yours.

Touch her other mother's heart, Lord, with the assurance that her child is well and happy. Let her know the joy her gift has brought, not only to us, but to a wide circle of relatives and friends.

Thank you for choosing me to be Laurie's mother. If I should ever meet her other one, give me the grace to share Laurie freely (I don't think I could do it on my own).

And thanks, especially, that Laurie and her friends liked my story!

"Thine eyes did see my substance, yet being unperfect; and in thy book all my members were written, which in continuance were fashioned, when as yet there was none of them" (Ps. 139:16, KJV).

Unloved, Unlovely, Unlovable

Today I found a letter Laurie had written when she was thirteen. In part, she said, "I dread every day. I'm barely passing my subjects. I'm not as pretty as my friends. Half the teachers hate me. I'm going downhill in basketball. Everytime I think about being dumb or not pretty enough, I start crying uncontrollably. Why is everything in life going wrong for me?"

That was Laurie's eighth-grade year. During that year she made the "B" Honor Roll each quarter and was a member of National Junior Honor Society; lettered in basketball and was on the starting team every game; was elected cheerleader by her fellow students; received the highest award possible on her music contest solo; and received an award (given by the teachers) for her contributions to school spirit and morale.

Laurie has matured some since then. She isn't quite as hard on herself now, or at least not down on herself as often. But those awful feelings of inferiority still plague her at times—and today is one of the times.

According to experts, Laurie's feelings aren't unusual. I once read that 98 percent of all teenagers feel dumb, ugly, friendless, and totally worthless at least part of the time. For lucky ones like Laurie, these moods are temporary. Other teens hurt every single day. Some even become suicidal. Actual facts don't seem to have much bearing on a teen's self-esteem: beautiful girls hate their looks, honor students berate themselves for being "stupid," talented athletes think they are too clumsy to compete.

Did I think Laurie would somehow (magically) escape the traumas common to other teens? She and I often talked about the physical changes that would take place, but I never even thought of discussing emotional upheavals.

I don't know what is wrong with Laurie. It could be anything or nothing. For the moment she's locked me out of her misery. There is nothing I can say or do right now.

But soon she will come out of her room, out of her shell. Would it help if I told her of the self-doubts that assailed me when I was her age? (Should I tell her about the time a boy called me "thunder thighs"? And how I hid my legs beneath voluminous skirts for the rest of the school year?) Perhaps I could remind her—again—that God loves her exactly as she is, imperfections and all, and that He has a divine purpose for her life.

Lord, until I can talk with her, please reach out and touch Laurie for me. Assure her she is loved and treasured by you, by us, by many others. Let her *feel* like the wonderful person she is!

Touch other teens who are in the same dark cavern. Don't let them feel forever unloved, unlovely, and unlovable. Replace those worthless, hopeless attitudes with the knowledge that, in you, each life is beautiful and good.

Lord, I want to add a prayer for parents whose children haven't yet entered adolescence. Prompt them to take, or make, time to talk about the great changes that will soon take place. Help them prepare their about-to-be-teens for the extreme mood swings and feelings of inferiority that are a part of growing up. Then, maybe, part of the awful stress and pain of being fifteen can be avoided.

"Yes, your cup of joy will overflow!" (John 15:11b).

Can You Baby-sit Tonight?

Against her better judgment and mine, Laurie is babysitting for the Jones family again tonight. They're the ones who like to stay out all night. But Laurie adores the children, Mrs. Jones pays top rates, and Laurie is broke. Besides, they *promised* to be home by midnight.

Laurie babysat for the first time when she was twelve—and still afraid to stay home alone.

"Babysitting is different!" she argued, when I wondered if she were old enough to accept the responsibility. "I won't be by myself! Toby will be with me!"

Toby was six months old. I think Laurie called me three

times that night, and I called her twice.

Before her second job, she took a Babysitter Safety Course. We both felt better knowing she was prepared to handle a tantrum, telephone the fire department, or give basic first aid.

The course helped us set some guidelines. Laurie only sits for families she knows or who can provide good references. She doesn't entertain friends while working unless the family (and I) knows and approves in advance. She won't sit a second time for people who won't pay the going rate or who return late without calling (except the Joneses). Safe transportation home must be provided, and she never, ever, gets into the car with a parent (or anyone else) who has been drinking. If a situation arises which she can't handle, she's to call home immediately.

Laurie's been fortunate. She's had only a few problems—all with parents, not children. She's been expected to clean house without instructions or extra pay. She's been left with sick youngsters (one mother "forgot" to tell Laurie her feverish child was prone to convulsions!). A few families haven't paid what they promised, or have failed to pay at all. And once Laurie was instructed not to sit in any of the living room chairs. "It bothers little Kay to see a stranger in Mommy's or Daddy's chair," the mother explained. "If you want to watch TV, either sit on the floor or bring a chair from the kitchen table."

Surely you understand, Lord, why I'm grateful for families who treat the babysitter with fairness and respect. Give those others (the minority, thank goodness) a new attitude toward those they hire to care for their children. Let them realize that babysitting is a respectable, responsible, and necessary job.

Be with Laurie tonight, Lord. Help her to be patient while she reads *Hop on Pop* for the tenth time. Help the baby go to sleep at a reasonable hour; last month he was cutting teeth and cried until midnight. Remind Laurie to go the extra mile, to wash that pile of dishes in the sink and perhaps straighten the living room.

And please, Lord, let the Joneses come home on time! If they don't, give Laurie the strength to say no next time they call.

"Let the children come to me, for the Kingdom of God belongs to such as they" (Mark 10:14).

The Right Answer

"I'm at the school," Laurie's voice came over the phone. "The party here is a real drag. There's another one going on at the Grove. Greg wants us to go out there."

The Grove is just that—some trees surrounding a small pond. It's a couple of miles out of town, and has been used for teenage parties for years. But there will be no adults there, and no restraints. Besides, this is Laurie's first date with Greg, and he is a senior.

"How late would you be?" I asked. "It's already ten-thirty."

"Oh, twelve or a little past."

"Who else is going?"

Laurie was vague. "Beth might go, and some of the others."

"What about kids already out of high school?" I continued.

"Mom, I can't predict who'll come and who won't!" There was a definite edge to Laurie's voice.

I was tempted to say yes. After all, Laurie wouldn't be at the Grove long. But I knew of several Grove gatherings that had gotten out of hand, and I wasn't sure anymore if this Greg was trustworthy.

"I don't think you'd better go," I said firmly. "If you explain that your date was for the school party, I'm sure Greg will understand."

Evidently he didn't. He brought Laurie home fifteen minutes later. I'd expected her to be angry and unhappy, but she wasn't.

"I was kind of hoping you wouldn't let me go," she said. "I don't think I would have been comfortable out there."

"Then why didn't you say no yourself?" I asked.

Laurie shrugged. "I don't know. Mainly because Greg's going on without me, and I don't like being left out. I really like him!"

When Laurie was younger, Lord, and faced with a situation she couldn't handle, she'd often whisper, "Say no, Mom—please!" Now she feels saying that difficult little word is her responsibility—and it is. Yesterday she turned down a skating invitation, explaining she was committed to a Christian fellowship car wash the same day. Last week she refused Mrs. Jones' plea to babysit, and she was frank about why (they didn't come home until 2:30 the last time Laurie was there!).

Still, there are times like tonight, when Laurie knows what she ought to do, but doesn't do it unless I tell her. Don't let me overprotect her, Lord. But when she gets cold feet and turns to me for help, let me be willing to give it. For her sake, give me the wisdom to know when the right answer is no.

"He shows how to distinguish right from wrong, how to find the right decision every time" (Prov. 2:9).

The Lie

Laurie lied to me today and I am furious! She told me she was going to the library with Beth and Kerri. And she did. Only Ted was there (by prearrangement) and instead of studying, she spent two hours cruising around in his car.

Laurie has always prided herself on being honest, on never saying things that aren't true. When I confronted her, she hotly defended her behavior. "I didn't lie!" she said angrily. "You didn't ask if Ted was going to be there. And you didn't tell me I had to stay at the library."

"Of course not!" I replied just as hotly. "I trusted you! It never entered my mind you would sneak around with Ted, then cover it up by lying. You know he isn't a suitable date or even friend."

"I think he is," she said, her voice cold and accusing. "And I didn't lie."

Surely Laurie realizes that lying consists of more than telling an untruth, even if she's too defensive to admit it right now. It's anything we say or do (or don't say or do) that is a deliberate attempt to deceive. It's quite possible to lie without making one false statement! We can tell only part of the story, for instance, or emphasize the side that is most favorable to us. For example, Lance once told me, truthfully, that another kindergartner had wandered off and gotten lost on the class trip to the circus. He didn't mention that he was with her!

Laurie is not an isolated case. A large number of Christian teens admit they have lied to stay out of trouble, to help a friend, or because they feel their parents place unreasonable demands on them. They know lying is a sin, and are usually sorry. But most say they will undoubtedly lie again.

There are probably very few teens who have never, ever, lied to their parents. I can remember doing it a couple of times when I was Laurie's age. I justified it by thinking, *My parents shouldn't ask things that are none of their business.*

But knowing how common lying is among teens isn't any help now. I'm angry, and I feel betrayed. In the back of my mind I keep wondering how many other times Laurie has deceived me. I am heartsick over her attitude, her adamant refusal to admit she was wrong.

Laurie's father and I have tried to make it easy for Lance and Laurie to be truthful. They've been taught from early childhood that God considers lying so serious that He included a prohibition against it in the Ten Commandments. We've been honest with them about family matters; we haven't glossed over our own mistakes and failures. We've tried to keep our expectations and standards reasonable, not making impossible demands for either behavior or performance. We've respected their rights to think differently from us.

We've tried to be open and truthful ourselves. Although, I confess, there have been many times when I failed, when I, too, lied. Sometimes I misrepresented the facts ever so slightly to make my point. Sometimes I exaggerated just a little to make myself look better. Sometimes I kept quiet when I should have spoken.

Cleanse me of my sin, Lord, so I can be free to help Laurie. She and I need to talk and pray, and settle not only the matter of lying but the disobedience that was behind it. We may not reach any conclusions—or not the same ones—but at least the matter will be out in the open instead of festering silently inside like a splinter buried deep in flesh.

Whatever happens, Lord, use your love to bridge this gap that has opened between us. Impress upon Laurie the serious, destructive consequences of lying, not only on her relationship with us, but on her relationship with you.

Let me be willing to forgive and forget; don't let me hold this lie forever against Laurie. Don't let it destroy the bonds of trust we've developed through the years.

"Stop lying to each other; tell the truth, for we are parts of each other and when we lie to each other we are hurting ourselves" (Eph. 4:25).

I Wish I Were Good

"Sometimes I wish I were like Beth," Laurie said the other day. "She's a genuinely good person."

"You're a good person, too, Laurie," I assured her. But I

knew what she meant. Beth has a gentle spirit; she seems to naturally, happily follow the right path.

Laurie is different. From birth she's accepted nothing without questioning, often challenging. "How do you *know* island is spelled with an 's'?" she asked her second-grade teacher. "It ought to be 'i-l-a-n-d'." In seventh grade she asked, "Can you prove it?" and today it's often, "Is that fair?"

She's mercurial, articulate, passionate—a modern Don Quixote. And it's not a bad way to be. This world needs more crusaders against injustice, more champions of right, maybe even more of those who wake people up and keep them on their toes. But these personality traits don't make life easy or comfortable—for Laurie or those around her.

For Laurie (and as you know so well, Lord, for me) being good, following you, is often an uphill climb. Laurie and I can identify with Paul's words in Rom. 7:21: "It seems to be a fact of life that when I want to do what is right, I inevitably do what is wrong."

We know we don't need to be slaves to our old, sinful natures. We've prayed . . . and prayed . . . and you are helping us both grow in grace. But, Lord, it seems to be a slow process. But by your grace we will become "those who follow after the Holy Spirit . . . doing those things that please God" (Rom. 8:5).

Laurie is so hard on herself. She wants to please us and to please you. When she fails she is devastated. I can only remind her that you helped shape our unique personalities (hers included) for your divine purposes. You made the gentle sheep who graze contentedly within the fence, and you made the mavericks who wriggle out between the wires.

I can also remind her that when you walked on earth, you chose some of those mavericks to be among the Twelve.

They turned the world upside down.

"Because of this light within you, you should do only what is good and right and true" (Eph. 5:9).

Today's Woman

"When I was your age," I told Laurie, "I wanted to backpack across the United States."

"Why didn't you?" she wondered.

"Because girls didn't do things like that. My mother would have had me committed if I'd even mentioned the idea."

Laurie laughed. "I think backpacking sounds fun! You can go after I graduate. Maybe I'll go with you."

It seems such a short time since I was Laurie's age. In some ways, though, it's been light years. Back then, being a woman was considerably more clear-cut than it is today. There were a lot of things (such as backpacking across the US) that most women simply didn't do. In fact, over 80 percent of us graduated from high school or college, perhaps worked briefly, then married and began a family—a family that would be our number-one priority even if we later returned to the marketplace.

Today it's different. Thousands of career opportunities have opened to women. Formerly "male" questions are now unisex: Should I choose college or vo-tech? What course of study? What career fields offer the advancement I want? Other questions remain primarily "women only": Can I do justice to both career and family? Should I have children early? Or wait until I am professionally established?

Laurie turns to me for answers I don't have. While I realize Christians are divided on the issue of a woman's role in society, I truly believe God offers us great freedom. I believe He loves and accepts those whose main interest is family, those who are devoted to a profession, and those who juggle both. He asks simply that these decisions be made with His guidance.

Thank you, Lord, for this fantastic freedom! At the same time, forgive me for the times I misused it, the times I was one-sided in counseling Laurie. I was so determined that she not be pushed into things traditionally "feminine" that I went overboard the other direction, warning her against burdening herself with tuna casseroles, runny noses, overflowing sinks, and the hundreds of other problems associated with family life. I didn't mention any of the hundreds of joys: love between husband and wife, a child's first step, the pleasure of a cup of coffee with a neighbor.

I don't think I've ever told Laurie how much I enjoy being a mother, how glad I am that my children came when I was young enough to enthusiastically, exuberantly share in their lives. I'll mention that at supper tonight, when we each recount a particular blessing or significant happening of the day. I'll add, too, that if I were starting my adult life again, I'd still choose family first, career second.

Even with the problems today's woman faces, I'm thankful Laurie is growing up at a time when she's free to pursue her dreams. Please, don't let her abuse this wonderful gift. Keep her growing in you, building a relationship that will last throughout eternity. Guide her dreams, that they may be lived in accordance with your will for her womanhood.

Thank you that Laurie didn't ridicule my own long-ago dream. Of course, I know that hiking across the United States is out of the question for us. But could we manage a week or two? Just Laurie and I?

Maybe we'll go this summer. We'd have fun, and there would be plenty of opportunities to talk, dream and pray. We'd have time alone with you, Father, time together to earnestly seek your will for Laurie's future.

"Live as those who are free to do only God's will at all times" (1 Pet. 2:16).

2

Eighteen at Last

It's the Law

Lance was home earlier than usual.

"Short track practice?" I asked.

"I didn't go," he told me. "I had to go to the post office before it closed."

"Why didn't you say something? I was there this morning and could—"

"Mom," Lance interrupted, giving me a long-suffering, where-have-you-been look, "I had to register for the draft. It's the law, remember?"

With that, he went about business as usual—as if declaring he was now of age to fight, kill, and die was something of no special importance. Was he really as casual as he sounded?

Maybe the possibility that war might actually touch us in the United States is so remote as to seem unreal. Or perhaps "growing up nuclear" has made him a fatalist, as I'm told many young people are. From birth, the shadow of the bomb has hung over them; worldwide destruction of life as we know it, whether by design or accident, is an all-too-real possibility.

We've talked about war and the draft. Our pastor has counseled Lance and others, explaining their options: register, refuse to register, or register and prepare to obtain conscientious objector status should they actually be drafted. I admire the courage of those young men who are being prosecuted for refusing to register. Lance and his father do not. Lance feels strongly that a Christian cannot ask to be exempt from what others must do. I respect this decision also, knowing it was guided by his faith in God.

Lance believes, as I do, that God is omnipotent, that He is aware of and involved with all that happens, personally and universally. I hope it's this belief that has allowed him to take this step so nonchalantly. I hope so, but I don't know. Increasingly, this handsome young man is a stranger to me.

Right now, Father, I wish he were a little boy again, playing cars or football or cowboys. I don't want him to be eighteen, to be old enough for war. I know I should trust you to take care of him, and I'm trying. Only it isn't easy.

Military service is no stranger to our family. Lance's father was serving in the army when we married. Two uncles have opted for military careers, and both are committed Christians. My own dad—the grandfather Lance never knew—was a pilot during World War II. But while that was a huge and horrible war, I believe it was fought for a just cause and fought to win.

Our nation's involvements since then have seemed much different. Vietnam has been considered an awful waste of young men and minds and resources. There is talk of the "morality" of war. I don't suppose any war is moral, but I'm sure some are more immoral than others.

Have we learned from our experience in past wars? Or are we doomed to repeat the lethal mistakes with each succeeding generation?

While I'm proud Lance is willing to do his part and serve our country, my whole being cries out to you, Lord. Spare him, merciful God! Spare our men and women from the horrors of war!

If there is something I can do to bring about peace, let

me do it without counting the cost.

"The Lord will settle international disputes; all the nations will convert their weapons of war into implements of peace. Then at last all wars will stop and all military training will end" (Isa. 2:4).

Am I a Man?

Ever since Lance turned eighteen, Lord, I've been wondering about something: when does a boy become a man?

In "primitive" societies it is easy to tell. Usually a boy has to pass a test—kill his first buffalo, for instance. Elaborate initiation rituals mark the transition and proclaim, "Today this boy becomes a man. From now on he will bear a man's responsibilities and enjoy a man's privileges."

There's no clear-cut dividing line for us. Even our legal age limits are fuzzy! Eighteen-year-olds can vote and go to war, but in some states they must wait additional years to marry without permission, enter into legal contracts, buy liquor, or run for public office.

Perhaps this lack of uniformity adds to the confusion some boys feel. Many try to prove their manhood through reckless driving, drinking, drugs, or even sleeping with as many girls as possible, then bragging about their exploits. In a way I can understand. This "macho man" image is portrayed as the norm by many movie, television, and sports heroes.

I know, Lord, (and I hope Lance does!) that these things have nothing to do with being a man. I'm grateful to Lance's dad for providing a very different pattern to follow. For eighteen years Lance has seen a man as someone who works steadily at a job he enjoys, serves God with his presence at worship on Sundays and with his lifestyle throughout the week, and who is always willing to help family or community.

Already Lance is assuming adult responsibilities. He registered for the draft and voted in last week's city elections. He's examining career possibilities, preparing to support himself and later a family. He's worked part time and summers for the past two years. He's developed some traits that will serve him well: honesty, punctuality, and giving whatever he does his best effort.

He even has a mature idea of what constitutes success. He wrote in an essay, "A man is successful if he's doing work he enjoys, even if it doesn't pay much, and if he's becoming the person God wants him to be."

I know, Lord, that there are times when Lance is tempted to prove himself in those less desirable ways. So when his image of what makes a man gets blurry and out of focus, bring to mind the real men he knows: his dad, our pastor, or that coach he admires. Let him follow their examples, as they follow yours.

Guide him, please, as he makes the transition from boy to man.

"But when I became a man my thoughts grew far beyond those of my childhood, and now I have put away the childish things" (1 Cor. 13:11b).

The College of His Choice

Is choosing a college more complicated now than it used to be? Maybe twenty-odd years have dimmed my memory, but I'm certain I applied to one school, was accepted, and that was that.

Lance's experience has been different. Part of the problem is that his career plans are uncertain. Computers captured his interest years ago, and he's taken every course the high school offered in programming. But it's a broad field, and Lance hasn't decided which phase to pursue. Because computers are relatively new to our lives, not all schools offer quality instruction. That's why the right choice is so important.

Should he go to State? It has a good program, but he wouldn't make the track team. What about our denominational school? They provide a caring, Christian atmosphere, but only a rudimentary computer course. Should Lance explore any of the dozens of schools which deluged him with brochures? (Including a Catholic seminary in the Midwest and a prominent women's college in the South!)

We talked for hours, weighing a dozen options. Lance spent a whole Saturday morning with the school's vocational counselor, and a Sunday evening talking with our pastor. The actual decision was a total surprise to me, and was announced casually over pizza.

"I'm going to North Community College next year," Lance said, poking a string of cheese into his mouth. "A guy from there talked to some of us at school last week. They liked my ACT scores, and will offer me an academic scholarship. Plus, I'm invited to try out for the track team."

"What about their computer department?" I asked, trying to conceal my shock. North is a fairly new school about 250 miles from here. It's small—under a thousand students—but other than that I don't know much about it.

"They claim to have the best program in the state, and the course catalog bears it out," Lance said, helping himself to another piece of pizza. "I've thought about it and prayed about it, and I'm certain North is the right choice. Everything seems to point there. Pastor called a nearby church and found out they have an active campus program."

"That's good," Lance's father said slowly. He was puzzled, and maybe a tiny bit hurt by Lance's decision. "I hear North is a good enough school. But are you *sure* you don't want to go to State? I loved it there!"

So did I. But Lance isn't his father and he isn't me. He first reminded me of that about ten years ago. We were spending the weekend at his grandmother's farm, and

Lance was spending all Saturday building a raft out of scrap lumber.

"The chances of that thing actually floating are about zero," I told him. "Besides, the pond is nearly dry. If I were you I wouldn't waste my time on that."

He weighed my suggestion, then answered calmly, "I'm not you. And I would."

Was it your doing, Lord? That it rained during the night, filling the pond? And that the raft not only floated, but supported Lance, Laurie, and Grandma's old dog, Sam?

Let me remember that experience as often as necessary in the days ahead. Lance is not me. He is not his father. His choices are no longer our choices. I guess that is as it should be.

I'm glad he didn't make this decision alone. Thank you for the help given by Pastor and by the school counselor, plus advice from people I don't know. Most of all, I'm grateful for your guidance, and that Lance has learned to rely on you.

Let him trust your guidance in a career choice, too. Help him recognize your guidance, whether it comes through a scripture passage, witness of another Christian, revelation of the Spirit, or (as in this) the open door.

Thank you that Lance has finally chosen a college. Let it be the right one—for you, for him, and for us.

"Wisdom and good judgment live together, for wisdom knows where to discover knowledge and understanding" (Prov. 8:12).

How Would You Rate This Room?

Lance and I drove to the college today, and we liked it. The campus is small and new. There are no sculptured gardens or vine-covered buildings, no ponderous air of scholarly tradition. But the classrooms are bright and airy, the grounds well-kept, and the tiny trees show promise of one day giving shade.

A friendly admissions officer, himself an alumnus, gave us a tour, treated us to lunch in the Student Union (the food was plentiful and not bad), and introduced several instructors. The students we talked with spoke highly of the school. I couldn't help but notice they had Lance's look—jeans, T-shirts, and running shoes.

The thing I liked best, though, was visiting the dormitories—living centers, they call them now. Each unit houses eight students, two to a bedroom, all sharing a bath and living area. When we opened the door to one, it was like stepping into Lance's room at home.

One end of the coffee table was piled high with books and magazines. Some playing cards covered the other end, and part of them had spilled over onto the floor. The wastebasket overflowed with empty pop cans, and not a single bed was made. Jeans were draped over the bedroom chairs. One young man evidently kept everything he owned—shirts, jeans, socks, towels and books—in a huge heap on his closet floor.

"How would you rate this room?" I asked the admissions officer.

"About average," he answered without hesitation. "It looks pretty messy, but it doesn't smell—no decaying Twinkies or moldy sandwiches lying around."

I was so relieved I could have hugged him.

A sparkling house has never been my top priority. I can ignore a messy desk or spilled-in oven or overflowing closet for a long time. However, I like neatness because I function better when things are orderly. For this reason, we have certain standards for the living areas of our home: used bath towels go in the hamper, not on the floor; no snack dishes are to be left on the kitchen counter; shoes and coats and school books don't belong in the living room (unless they are being worn or studied).

But other than insisting that their clothes be properly

cared for (clothing is too expensive to be ruined through carelessness or neglect), I've made Lance's and Laurie's rooms their own responsibility. And while Laurie does a good job, I wasn't sure Lance's idea of a clean room would satisfy the college.

Years ago, a friend shared her formula for teaching children how to help around the house. First, the parent explains what needs to be done and gives clear instructions for doing it, making sure the child understands. Next, the parent insists the job be finished correctly. If necessary, he gives physical assistance. (Once, during the learning process, my big hand gripped Laurie's tiny one as she picked up at least twenty toys and put them in the toy box. But we didn't stop until the job assigned—picking up toys—was complete. The next time she did it by herself.) Last, the parent praises a job well done.

The formula worked then and it works now. Lance and Laurie can do the basic cooking, laundry, and cleaning that must be done around a house—at least around our house. Except for Lance's messy room, they do an acceptable job.

Maybe I was silly, Father, but I do feel much better now. Lance's housekeeping habits won't cause his roommate to throw up, nor the houseparents to ask, "What kind of mother does that kid have?" Lance is not filthy, nor is he picky-clean. And I've discovered he is average, very much like the majority of his peers.

While he's still home, Lord, I think I'll simply close his door.

"A time to find; a time to lose; a time for keeping; a time for throwing away" (Eccles. 3:6).

The Kold Kube Kid

Lance met my car when it pulled into the drive. "I've got a job!" he announced jubilantly, grabbing two sacks of groceries to carry in. "I start tomorrow morning at 8:00."

"Lance, that's wonderful! **Where?**"

"Kold Kube Ice Company. **Mr. Bricke** called right after you left and said the job was mine if I wanted it. I'll bag, load, and deliver ice all over the county."

"Didn't you apply there earlier?" I asked. "I thought Jason's cousin had been hired."

"He quit. Didn't like the schedule. We're off Tuesday and Sunday, but work ten or twelve hours every Saturday. I'll also have to work July Fourth." Lance set the groceries on the counter, took a candy bar from one of the sacks, and devoured it in three bites. "Guess who's going to be my main helper? Mr. Bricke's kid—the one who talks ninety miles an hour."

"Think you can handle being with him all day?"

"I hope so. I'm sure going to try."

Whatever the drawbacks (and every job has some), I'm so thankful Lance has found work. He'd expected to work at Green's Grocery again; he has the past two summers. Their unexpected closing left him high and dry, for most other jobs had already been snapped up. He was beginning to get very discouraged, not to mention short of money.

Lord, help Lance take today's enthusiasm with him onto the job. Thank you for the work experience that has taught him to be prompt and dependable. I guess more people get fired over those two things than almost anything else. I'm glad Lance is strong enough to do heavy work, and that he's willing to give up his Saturdays.

It occurs to me, Lord, that this job may be the answer to more prayers than one. You know Lance is short of patience; he's brought the problem before you several times. Maybe spending the summer with a motor-mouthed twelve-year-old is just the thing he needs to help him develop this vital trait.

So help him, please, to be tolerant and understanding—and to keep his cool!

"We can rejoice, too, when we run into problems and trials for we know that they are good for us—they help us learn to be patient" (Rom. 5:3).

My Car Won't Start

Lance's car wouldn't start this morning. He checked all the obvious things: gas gauge, battery, starter wires. Nothing appeared wrong, but the engine adamantly refused to turn over.

He was upset, and so was I. Although he's had the use of our ancient pickup for driving to school and work, this is the first car he's owned and he's rightfully proud of it! Buying it was a family project: his grandparents and we paid half as a graduation gift, and he's paying the rest from salary and savings. The car is only a few months old, and certainly shouldn't have quit.

I think Lance hoped I would call and make arrangements for having the car repaired. I didn't offer. It's his car, and he should handle it. Shouldn't he?

At any rate, when Lance called the shop foreman, he was told it would be at least three days before anyone could even look at it, and then we'd need to have it towed in. Lance then insisted on speaking to the manager.

"The car is new, under warranty, and I bought it partly because I believed your claims of 'satisfaction guaranteed,'" he said firmly but politely. "I need the car to get to my job, and I expect someone to find out what's wrong and repair it today."

He took my car to work. Less than an hour after he'd left, a mechanic drove up and replaced a defective alternator.

I was glad that Lance showed maturity in handling this situation. He didn't become angry, but he did insist that promises of satisfactory service be honored.

Thank you, Lord, that this attitude carries over into his

driving habits. Why do some teens (and adults, to be fair) equate fast or reckless driving with being a real man or woman? Some even boast about the number of warnings or speeding tickets they've received.

One of Lance's friends has wrecked three cars already. His injuries have been minor, and each time his parents have shelled out money for another vehicle. Maybe it's a blessing our family doesn't have that kind of cash.

Two more of his classmates would be looking forward to college now if they hadn't been driving 85 miles per hour on a rural road. The car hit some loose gravel and flipped twice. One of the boys was killed outright, the other's life still hangs in the balance. No amount of money can buy back a life or repair a mangled body.

Help Lance and his friends to be careful, responsible drivers. Let them see traffic laws and those who enforce them for what they are: a protection for us all.

And thanks that Lance's car is fixed so I can have mine back!

"Patience is better than pride! Don't be quick-tempered—that is being a fool" (Eccles. 7:8a, 9).

The Wreck

"Mom?" Lance's voice came over the telephone one Sunday afternoon. "I have bad news. I've wrecked my car."

My heart nearly stopped. "Are you okay? Is anyone hurt? Where are you?"

"I'm fine, not even a scratch. I sideswiped a mailbox, and the car is a mess." His voice broke. "I'm at Beth's. Can you and Dad pick me up?"

I don't know what I expected to see. I guess I thought Lance would be covered with blood and the car in a ditch. Instead, it was parked in Beth's driveway, with Lance, Beth, and her parents gathered around it.

"It was totally my fault," Lance said.

"What happened?" his dad asked.

"I noticed some water dripping out from under the dash. I leaned down to see where it was coming from, and the next thing I knew I'd hit the mailbox and was headed for the sidewalk." Lance was nearly in tears. "How could I have been so stupid?"

"We're just glad no one was hurt," I told him. I was weak with relief. "The car can be fixed."

We didn't scold Lance; he felt bad enough already. The expense and inconvenience of repairing the mailbox and car would make this a lesson he wouldn't forget. At the same time, we wondered if we'd done enough to make sure Lance knew safe driving practices.

Less than 8 percent of the licensed drivers in the United States are teenagers, yet they account for over twice that many accidents. Alcohol and drug abuse is a factor; over half the teen drivers killed show alcohol in their blood. But other accidents occur because the young driver didn't know or didn't apply safety practices most of us have learned through experience.

Their dad spent several hours driving with Lance and Laurie (she has her learner's permit and will be getting a regular license soon) to reinforce the lessons they'd learned in Driver's Education. Lance needed no reminder about the most basic rule: never take your eyes off the road. A fraction of a second of inattention is enough to cause an accident.

They went to an auto salvage dealer to look at tires. Seeing the bald tires on mangled vehicles was enough to convince them to either spend money on good tires or not drive at all. They also saw a demonstration of the "jaws of life," used to free victims (or bodies) from damaged cars.

Impatience is a factor in many accidents. Young drivers caught behind a slow-moving vehicle often pass when they shouldn't, with fatal results. Or, irritated by a driver who doesn't dim his lights, they flash their own brights. Then both drivers are blind. Lance and Laurie practiced watching the edge of the road instead of looking directly into the lights of an oncoming car; both said it helped.

Lord, I thank you that Lance wasn't hurt. Thank you for the lesson he learned, and for the lessons my husband took time to teach. Be with Lance, Laurie, and the millions of other teenage drivers on our streets and highways. Let them remember that driving is a privilege, not a right, and that it must not be abused.

Let them imagine you as their passenger, Lord. If everyone did, the accident rate would fall to practically zero.

"I will continue to teach you those things which are good and right" (1 Sam. 12:23b).

Do I Have What It Takes?

Several years ago I knew a boy whose severe learning disabilities kept him from learning to read. Although he was bright and talented in other areas, he suffered spells of acute depression because of his "dumbness." When he was about ten he told his parents, "I've decided to try and enjoy life as much as I can until I'm eighteen. Then I'll kill myself."

"Why?" his mother asked, trying to conceal her shock.

"Because I can never be a man," he explained. "I can't read, so I can't get a job. Without a job I can't get married or have children, because I couldn't support them. I can't vote, pay bills, read the newspaper, or do any of the things men do."

Fortunately, before he was eighteen, he was able to overcome his handicap.

Lance has no such problem. He can read and write—and do calculus and physics and trigonometry. He has an enviable record of school and sports successes behind him. Still, he sometimes worries about his capacity to fulfill adult responsibilities. He wonders if he has what it takes to be a man in today's world.

When he was younger, Lance was self-confident almost to the point of being cocky. He saw himself as a wonderful, likable, competent person.

A few days after he started kindergarten he announced, "I'm the biggest kid in my class."

"Oh?" Unless I'd missed someone, Lance was about the smallest child. "What about Jason and Tina and Mark?"

"Oh, they're taller and weigh more," he admitted, "but I'm still the biggest. Ask anyone."

At that age there was nothing Lance couldn't do. No mountain was too high, no ocean too wide, no desert too hot. Setbacks? They were of little importance.

I remember asking about a footrace his class had run.

"I was last," he told me cheerfully. "But I was a good last."

Time and disappointments have tempered Lance's self-image, Lord, and I guess that's natural. Now, though, he needs some of that old confidence back. Could you, please, restore a little of it?

Maybe I can help, too, by remembering the power of praise. Tonight, I'll compliment him for that "A" in Physics (and acknowledge the effort it required). I'll be more appreciative of his willingness to drive Laurie here and there and everywhere.

Instead of taking Lance for granted, I'll let him know how very glad I am that he is my son!

"And yet you have made him only a little lower than the angels, and have placed a crown of glory and honor upon his head" (Ps. 8:5).

3

Our Family Circle

Time to Eat

Family meals look so enticing on television. Everyone is smiling. No matter what Mother has prepared, the food is greeted with choruses of "Wow!" or "My favorite!" In between bites, there's time for meaningful conversation among family members.

Many articles by Christian writers portray mealtime in much the same light. Parents use the time to teach about God and to impart worthwhile values to their children (who are, of course, properly trained and receptive).

Sometimes our meals are like that. Sometimes we discuss morality, the Middle East, miracles, and whether the Shroud of Turin is real.

But there are other times, too, and tonight will probably be one of them. We're having meatloaf, Lance's favorite main dish. Laurie, however, thinks it's "disgusting," a word she also uses to describe chicken, pork, tamales, rabbit, asparagus, tomatoes, and a hundred other things.

Lance has always been a hearty eater. While he has been known to fill his cheeks with grapes and announce "I'm a chipmunk," or let a strand of spaghetti hang from the corner of his mouth and wait for Laurie's horrified reaction, he spends most of his table time eating.

Laurie, by contrast, can think of a thousand things to do

with food besides eating it. At one, she enjoyed spooning it into her hair or dropping it onto the floor for the cat. At three, she painted pictures on the plate with catsup and refused jello because "it isn't dead yet." At ten, she blew a mouthful of peas across the table at her father, resulting in her last spanking.

She's made a lot of progress. She holds Lance's hand during the blessing without yelling, "But he has germs! I might get them!" She doesn't complain about the meals (much), and tough basketball practices have increased her appetite while reducing the number of foods she dislikes. Still, I can count ten recent times when she's eaten all she wanted in three minutes flat, then spent the remainder of the meal twisting, twirling, talking nonstop, or otherwise entertaining.

Are there other families like ours, Lord? Have we somehow missed the mark?

Maybe I should stop thinking about the bad things and thank you for the good ones. In some families, each person fills a plate from the stove and eats whenever and wherever he chooses; at least we do eat together once or twice a day. And blessings abound! Laurie has been on time for breakfast every day for two weeks. Friends have commented on our children's excellent table manners and good eating habits (Lance and Laurie evidently save their worst behavior for home). We've certainly established what someone called "the tradition of mealtime talk," although it may revolve around whether the Cowboys will win the Superbowl this year. Or what happened in ball practice. Or what the principal said to a certain teacher when he thought no one heard.

You, Lord, are the unseen guest at every meal. Help us—all of us—to act as though you were physically present each time we eat. Let these mealtimes nourish our spirits as well as our bodies.

Tonight, Lord, I'd really appreciate it if you would let Laurie see only the scalloped potatoes—not the meatloaf.

"As they sat down to eat, he asked God's blessing on the food and then took a small loaf of bread and broke it and was passing it over to them, when suddenly—it was as though their eyes were opened—they recognized him!" (Luke 24:30, 31a).

Thank You, Alexander Graham Bell

Social commentators note that where hairstyles and clothing are concerned, only superficial differences exist between the sexes. At our house, however, a man from Mars could tell the boy from the girl: all he'd have to do is observe the differences in their telephone behavior.

Lance answers the phone under one of four conditions: he is within arm's reach; he is the only one home; I ask him to; or he wants to tease Laurie. While he occasionally talks at length to Jason, Kim, or Mark, most of his conversations are short.

"Kim?" he'll say. "I have to work late tomorrow, so I'll pick you up at seven instead of six. Okay? Good. See you then."

Laurie's actions are just the reverse. "I'll get it!" she yells the moment the phone rings. Simultaneously, she dashes for my bedroom (location of one of our phones). If the call is for her, and it usually is, she sprawls across the bed, turns on the radio, then proceeds to talk in muted tones to Beth, Kerri, Mike or whomever. The conversation usually continues until I yell, "Laurie! You've been on ten minutes!" Her standard response is "Just a second. This is urgent." At that point, I give her three more minutes before insisting she hang up.

Lord, the telephone is truly one of the wonders of modern life. At the same time, its blessings can easily be abused. Let me always be courteous on the telephone, and teach Laurie and Lance to do the same.

Help me to stand firm in insisting they follow our guidelines regarding telephone use. We have a ten- (or thirteen-) minute limit on most calls. Of course there are occasions when we talk longer, but this rule prevents two-hour tie-ups and keeps us from missing important calls. For the same reasons, we let the phone "rest" a few minutes between calls. Both Lance and Laurie know we expect their friends to identify themselves when asked, instead of giggling or hanging up; and we ask them to do the same when they make calls.

I started teaching proper answering etiquette when Laurie was three, right after I reached the phone too late to keep her from hanging up, but in time to hear her say, "Hello, silly person! I'm home all by myself." I've settled for a polite "Hello." The more formal "Hello, this is Lance speaking" was more than I could manage.

A cartoon in last week's paper pointed to another problem that comes up: messages, or lack of them. The businessman father asked, "Who on earth is this Mr. Mxbpth who called on urgent business?" The teenage son shrugs and says, "I dunno. The name sounded strange to me too."

We've had our share of strange, unreadable messages. Once Laurie tried to excuse herself by saying, "I was too embarrassed to ask him to repeat his name a third time." Now she and Lance know they must get the name correctly, even if they must ask that it be spelled. They also must ask whether the person will call again or wishes the call returned, and they are supposed to write everything down.

Most of the time they remember, except last week. Lance told me I was supposed to call Grandma right back—three days after her original call.

I've got to go now, Lord. Laurie's been on the telephone thirteen minutes plus. But regardless of the problems, thank you for this marvelous instrument! With it, I can easily and often "reach out and touch" those I love.

"Let your conversation be gracious as well as sensible,

for then you will have the right answer for everyone" (Col. 4:6).

Cyclops

It was one of those rare, "do-nothing" afternoons for Laurie.

"Why don't you play tennis?" I suggested.

"There's no one to play with," she told me. "Beth is at her grandma's, and Kerri went to the orthodontist."

"Are those your only friends?" I prodded.

So Laurie made three calls, and received three no's. It seems that most teenage girls have standing afternoon dates with *General Hospital* and *Edge of Night*.

"See, Mom?" Laurie said, half triumphantly. "We really are the only family in the world that doesn't watch soaps."

We're not, I'm sure. But the incident made me think about the place television has in our lives. It can be a wonderful blessing. Countless people have heard the gospel and accepted Christ as Savior through this media. It provides companionship and a link with the outside world for millions of people who are homebound, sick, or elderly. It expands our horizons; through it we can travel, meet people around the world, and experience some of the best in music, sports, and the arts.

But television can also be a menace. So many programs (and advertisements) are not only silly, but give a warped picture of life as God intended it to be! We are bombarded with messages: love conquers all; sex appeal should be our goal in life; if it feels right, do it; football heroes get the beautiful girls and live happily ever after.

Watching television is also a passive experience, and it's easy to get into the habit of sitting in front of the set. I remember a birthday party Laurie attended when she was nine. The guest of honor opened her gifts, then spent the next two hours watching television. She wouldn't join in any of the games, and even ate her cake and ice cream with eyes glued to the screen.

Our family isn't free of TV-related problems. Laurie loves "romantic" movies and situation comedies, no matter how mindless. Lance, if he has time, will watch any sport—sumo wrestling to boat racing—until his eyes cross. And I rush through Sunday dinner on days when the Dallas Cowboys are playing an early game.

But I'm grateful that the Holy Spirit gave me guidance (and strength) to set strict controls on television watching when Lance and Laurie were young. They had to ask permission to turn on the set, and were allowed only selected programs and a limited amount of viewing. Sometimes I turned off unsuitable shows in the middle. We made it our policy to eat most meals at the table, without the television. These early rules have kept television a minor issue now that the children are teens.

I no longer exercise rigid controls. They are free to choose what and how much they will watch, within limits (last night I turned off a movie that was trashy and tasteless). But I have mixed feelings about censorship. I know we watch programs that some Christians find objectionable or downright indecent. For instance, my husband and I felt the subject matter and opportunities for discussion provided by the mini-series *Holocaust* far outweighed the moments of nudity, profanity, and violence. Still, I wonder, *Am I too strict? Too lenient?*

Give me your perspective, Lord, about this modern miracle-menace. Let me guide the children's selections without setting myself up as a blue-nose censor or self-appointed critic of taste. Thank you that Lance and Laurie are exercising self-discipline in this area, so that the one-eyed Cyclops doesn't dominate their lives.

By the way, Lord, I played tennis with Laurie since no one else would. I'm too slow and rusty to give her a good game, but we both had fun. Over iced tea afterward, she admitted it had the soaps beat by a mile.

"Learn as you go along what pleases the Lord" (Eph. 5:10).

Let's (Don't) Go Skiing

For the third year in a row I've lost the family vacation battle. We'll be going on the church ski trip again instead of somewhere (anywhere!) warm and dry.

It's not that I can't ski. I can. I can handle most intermediate slopes and some advanced ones. But I've never learned to like it. It's dangerous, for one thing. Few sports boast as many broken legs and twisted ankles. I worry about Lance and Laurie. They tackle the most difficult "experts only" runs at breakneck speeds! Yet my husband quietly assures me they are competent, safe skiers in complete control!

I hate cold weather. My fingers and toes are numb from October until June, and my lips turn blue at the *thought* of snow. On last year's trip we skiied in a mini-blizzard. My eyelashes actually froze together while I rode the lift, blinding me until I could pry them apart.

I guess vacations never satisfy everyone, everytime. So I'll stop complaining and thank the Lord for the wonderful times our family has had in the past, and for the memories we've built. We'll always remember the Christmas we went to Disney World (in warm, sunny Florida). We stayed, fascinated by everything, from opening until late-night holiday closing. Laurie, just five, still had energy to challenge Lance with, "I'll race you to the car!"

Besides trips for the family, we try to spend a few days alone—husband and wife. Parental pressures are still there even when the children reach their teens, so parents have the same need to get away as they did earlier. It's easy to become so absorbed in our children we forget that the core of the family is the couple. We began as two, we'll end as two. Far too many marriages break apart when the children grow up and leave home. Counselors say that it's often because husband and wife neglected to keep in touch and grow with each other.

Just last year I accompanied my husband on a business trip to San Diego (warm and sunny there too). Not only did we have a wonderful visit with my brother and his family, but I had four days alone to explore that marvelous and multi-faceted city—plus ample chance to learn about freeway driving. We had long evenings together to become reacquainted and refreshed. I'll treasure that trip for a long time.

Right now, though, everyone else is looking forward to skiing, Lord, so I'll try to adjust my attitude to match. Thank you for the upcoming vacation. We'll be a family among other families who make up your body, and we'll have unique opportunities for fun and fellowship. Help me be a good sport. Let me understand the joy others find in skiing. Don't let me dampen their high spirits or chill their good times by my lack of enthusiasm.

I'll honestly try to enjoy the sport. It would help, Lord, if we could have at least one day when the wind didn't blow and the temperature was above 15°.

"...and there was warm fellowship among all the believers" (Acts 4:33b).

She Doesn't Like Me Today

This hasn't been a good afternoon. I had a meeting right after lunch, so I asked Laurie to wash the dishes and clean up the kitchen. When I got home the lunch things were still on the table. The stove was greasy, the skillets and pans piled in the sink. Laurie was simultaneously talking on the telephone, watching television, and painting her toenails.

"Sorry about the mess," she apologized casually after I turned off the TV and made her hang up the phone. "Beth called right after you left, then I got interested in a ball game, then a minute ago Greg called. But I'll get everything done right now."

She cleaned up, but I had to call her back twice to do things she forgot. She knew I was annoyed, but not ten minutes later she interrupted an article I was trying to finish.

"Greg wants me to go with him to a party in the city," she said. "Is it okay with you?"

"Who's giving it?" I wanted to know. "Have you met them?"

Laurie shook her head. "No, but Greg says they're nice."

"When is it?"

"Tonight. We'd need to leave about six."

"Where do they live?"

"I told you, in the city!" Laurie replied impatiently. "I don't know the street address, if that's what you mean."

"That's exactly what I mean." I matched her tone of voice. "You don't know the people. You don't know where they live. You probably don't know what kind of party it's going to be. Well, you ought to know without asking that you can't go."

"Why? Because you don't like Greg? Because you don't trust me?"

"Trust has to be earned, Laurie!" I snapped. "I can't even trust you to do the dishes."

"You are unreasonable and sometimes I don't like you at all!" she shouted.

I had to bite my tongue to keep from saying, "Sometimes I don't like you either."

Laurie stalked off to her room. She came out for supper, but only because her father insisted. She ate in total silence, lifting her eyes from her plate only long enough to give me a couple of hostile stares.

Laurie did act irresponsibly this afternoon, but so did I. I violated three cardinal rules for settling disagreements: I lost my temper; I didn't stick to the issue (We were discussing a party, but I was angry about the dishes, so brought them up when they had no place in the discussion.); and I gave Laurie a flat no without helping her think through the situation.

Laurie knows she can attend only parties that are chaperoned and are given by friends we know. My answer probably would have been the same, but I could have given her the opportunity to search out details: who, where, what kind of party, the names of adults present. It's possible Laurie could have attended. At any rate, we probably could have avoided this unpleasant afternoon.

Late tonight Laurie came and sat on the edge of my bed. "I wasn't very nice today, was I?" she asked in a small voice.

My heart went out to her. For a moment she was three again, looking up at me with sorrowful eyes and saying, "Laurie's been a bad girl, Mama."

"I didn't handle the situation very well either," I told her. "I'm really sorry."

"I'm sorry, too," she said.

I reached over and hugged her. "Tomorrow's a brand new day, and we'll both do better."

She laughed. "You always say that! Ever since I was little!"

Tomorrow. Dear Lord, I thank you that tomorrow is a new, fresh day, and that Laurie and I can start all over again. Most especially I thank you for the bond of love that sustains and strengthens us even when we fight—even on days like this, when we really don't like each other.

"Great is his faithfulness; his lovingkindness begins afresh each day" (Lam. 3:23).

Death in the Family

Something happened last night that has our whole family shaken to the core: Laurie's old cat, Josie, was murdered.

Laurie found her on the porch this morning, her head and tail cleanly severed from the body. How I wish I could have spared Laurie that frightening, sickening sight! She was wild with shock and grief! So was I, but my sorrow was overshadowed by a chilling fear. Who would have—could have—done such a horrible thing? And why? Did someone have a grudge against Laurie, and used this to get even? Would they try to harm her?

Thank goodness for my husband's steadying presence. He called the police while Laurie and I stood with our arms around each other and cried. The call set our minds at ease about Laurie's safety; this was the fourth identical incident reported. The cat mutilations were apparently at random, and an investigation was underway.

The death of one small cat is insignificant when compared with the carnage and destruction that is a fact of life in war-torn parts of our world. But the Creator and Lord of all things surely understands the special relationship between a girl and her cat.

Josie wandered up to our house years ago, a scraggly, starving grey kitten. Laurie immediately adopted her, and from the beginning Josie was Laurie's devoted companion.

I have a picture of Laurie and Beth wheeling a dressed-up Josie around the yard in a doll buggy. There's a faint stain on Laurie's rug where Josie accidentally knocked over one of the innumerable tiny cups of chocolate milk she received as "honored guest" at tea parties. During Laurie's vegetarian binge, Josie grew fat on meat meant for her owner.

Laurie has grown up, Josie had grown old. Lately, Josie spent much of each day dozing on her special pillow at the foot of Laurie's bed. Nights she curled up in her box in the garage, or stalked imaginary mice in the yard. When the kitchen light came on each morning, Josie would jump on the screen and meow her desire to come in. Until today.

Laurie couldn't bear to touch the mutilated body, so Lance carefully wrapped Josie in an old baby blanket. He called Beth and Mark, and the four of them left a few minutes ago to bury Josie in Mark's grandpa's orchard.

Please, Father, let Laurie feel your special, comforting presence. Touch her with your care and concern. Heal any emotional damage, and help her remember only the love she and Josie shared.

Remind me to stand back and give Laurie time to grieve, for that is an integral part of the healing process. Keep me from the temptation to provide another pet to take away the pain; when she's ready for another kitten, Laurie will let me know.

This part of my prayer is so much harder, Lord. Help me to forgive those responsible for this awful act, and help Laurie to forgive them too. Be with the police as they search for the guilty parties, not so much that they may be punished, but that they may be helped. Surely these killings came from twisted minds.

Comfort the others who lost precious pets. Let this death, tragic and needless as it is, make me a more compassionate, loving person, better able to extend your love to others who grieve.

"What is the price of five sparrows? A couple of pennies? . . . . Yet God does not forget a single one of them" (Luke 12:6).

I Wish They'd Known Dad

My uncle visited today. He'd come with some friends to do a little hunting. But he isn't really a hunter and the weather was cold and damp, so he spent his time with us.

Lance and Laurie sat entranced as he told stories that began in one of two ways: "When your mother was a little girl. . . ," and "Your grandfather and I. . . ."

Dad died the year I was eighteen, after a long and terrible struggle with cancer. He never met my husband, never saw my children. It's times like this, remembering, when I realize how much Lance and Laurie have missed by not knowing him.

He was partial to little girls. Laurie, with her elfin grace and dancing eyes, would have captured his heart as completely as she did ours. She, like Dad (and me), is a voracious reader. The world of books would have bound them close.

Dad and Lance would have had some battles. They are much alike, both impatient and often intolerant, but generous to a fault and willing to go to any length to help a person in need. Dad would have loved watching Lance run. He loved sports, but worked his way through school and wasn't able to participate when he was young.

In his heart and spare time, Dad was a poet. Both children share his love of the written word. Just yesterday, Lance read two versions of a theme he was writing. "Which wording is best?" he asked. Tears came to my eyes as I remembered the times Dad asked my mother the very same question.

Grandparents are so important. I'm thankful, God, that my mother has taken an active role in Lance and Laurie's lives. My heart goes out to children who miss the rich heritage grandparents can offer. So often parents limit the contact, and for silly, superficial reasons. Please, Lord, don't let them get hung up over things grandparents do that are different. Let them, instead, do everything possible to encourage the fulfilling, almost mystical relationship between young and old.

My grandparents were special, and their influence is with me to this day. Grandma patiently taught me to play the old gospel hymns on her piano—"When the Roll Is Called Up Yonder," "Down at the Cross," "Wonderful Words of Life." Lord, I never play them in church without thanking her, and you, in my heart. My grandfather taught me to ride on Spot, the twenty-seven-year old horse my youngest aunt rode when she was a child. I still enjoy riding today. Once Grandpa bought a little cart and goat, just for me. Grandma made us sell them after "Morning Glory" destroyed every one of her precious flower beds. But the memory brings a smile to my heart.

When I think of my uncle's stories, the word "bittersweet" comes to mind. According to Webster, it means "pleasure alloyed with pain." That's a perfect description of today. Still, I thank you for it. In a small way, my uncle helped Lance and Laurie know their grandfather. Even though many of the memories are painful, it's worth the cost.

I've never been to visit my father's grave, Lord. Not once. Now I think I'm ready. This Memorial Day we'll make the trip—Lance, Laurie, their father and I.

"Let each generation tell its children what glorious things [Jehovah] does" (Ps. 145:4).

Christmas at Church

The church is hushed. The only light comes from the soft glow of candles. It's so peaceful here I almost wish I could stay forever.

With a family, sometimes it seems that life is a frantic rush from one activity to another, from one problem to the next. Right now Lance has girlfriend problems and is trying to handle a ton of physics homework every night—while coping with his resentment toward the teacher.

Laurie is having problems with Laurie. She makes impossible demands on herself, which take a severe toll on her temper and self-esteem.

In a world where so many have real and crushing troubles, ours are small. And so, Lord, I thank you for them. For which of us would actually choose another's problems in place of our own? I know the vacation from school and sports and business will work wonders in restoring our bodies and spirits. Help us use the time to rest and renew, to regain our sense of balance.

The organ begins the strains of "Silent Night," and I forget my worries. As I look at the Christmas tree—a lovely, living green decorated with gold and white symbols of your life—I am lost in wonder. How much you loved us to leave heaven and live among us on earth!

The program begins with the high, happy voices of young children singing "Away in a Manger." Then comes a pageant. Lance is reading the Scripture narration from the book of Luke. His voice is deep, clear, confident. As I listen, I'm assured that our current struggles are a part of our growth in you, Christ. You will guide us through this next year as you have all the years that are past.

The spotlight focuses on the manger, and Laurie begins singing a lullaby. Her voice is so true and clear it brings tears to my eyes. You know things aren't always easy for us or between her and me, Lord. When we're in conflict, let this song echo in my heart, reminding me of the joy she brings.

Dear Jesus, thank you for this Christmas program and the spiritual calm it is bringing to my soul. Thank you for the friends, family and neighbors who are worshiping with me; their presence makes me feel less alone. Most especially, thank you for coming on that long-ago Christmas eve. Thank you for being God's special gift to us.

"I bring you the most joyful news ever announced, and it is for everyone! The Savior—yes, the Messiah, the Lord— has been born tonight in Bethlehem!" (Luke 2:10b, 11).

4

Two by Two

Is Dating Okay?

Lance and Laurie were snickering when they came home from school.

"Mom, you should have heard this radio preacher," Laurie told me. "You'd have cracked up."

"Laurie was fooling with the dial and picked up a program from California," Lance explained. "Someone had written in to ask if it was a sin for Christian kids to date."

"Christian *young people*," Laurie corrected with mock primness.

"Christian young people," Lance parroted. "The preacher said he generally disapproved of dating, and felt God did, too."

"Did he give reasons?" I asked.

Laurie shook her head. "The station faded out. He was probably from one of those fringe groups that is opposed to everything."

I started to agree, then remembered a friend of mine. She believes God has mates selected for each of us; by dating, we take control out of God's hands and hinder His perfect plan. I told Lance and Laurie about her. "I imagine there are other Christians who feel the same way."

They were unimpressed by that view. I confess I also have trouble thinking of God as a divine matchmaker, although I know He is vitally concerned with our selection of mates. But the incident did provide a springboard for some talk about modern dating.

Much of the discussion centered around people Lance and Laurie know—the girl who will go out with anyone just to say she has a date; the boy who collects girls like baseball cards. All in all, we charted a number of wrong reasons for dating: to get sexual favors; to appear popular; to be like everyone else; or to have someone be exclusively yours—Laurie calls it "a romantic security blanket."

The right reasons? To have fun, to get to know a wide variety of people, and to become well acquainted with a person.

Lance concentrates on the fun part. He's usually dating, or liking, two or three girls at any given time. Laurie thinks dating more than one person at a time is creepy. "You date a guy to get to know him," she says. "It's funny how it works out, though. Sometimes the better you know someone, the more you like him. Other times, when you find out how a person really thinks and acts, the attraction totally disappears."

Lord, thank you for helping Lance and me control the temptation to say, ". . . like with Ted?" Laurie isn't seeing him now, and I'm truly grateful. But there will be other unsuitable boys, and I ask you to help me keep calm, to let her see them, but only in controlled situations such as church or home. Help Laurie to understand that these restrictions are for her own protection.

Be with Lance as he dates. Don't let him concentrate exclusively on fun, especially his own fun. Let him take time to really know the girls he takes to dinner, for tennis, or to a game.

Bless that radio preacher, Lord, and the person who wonders if dating is a sin. My own conscience is free on that point; properly used, dating is a valuable experience. I have plenty of other questions, though. Guide me as we deal with those problems in our family, and be with other families going through the same process.

Above all, keep Lance and Laurie and their friends aware that in their dating lives, as in every other part, your standards should be upheld, your name glorified.

"But be sure in deciding these matters that you are living as God intended. . ." (1 Cor. 7:17a).

Rules for the Dating Game

Lance and Laurie have dates tonight. Lance took Susie to a movie, and Greg picked Laurie up ten minutes ago to go bowling. I'm alone in the kitchen, staring at the remains of lasagne and thinking about how this business of dating begins.

My own first date was one of many memorable, miserable evenings during my teen years. My date's mother drove us to and from a church wiener roast. During the party he ignored me totally; in the car we sat as far apart as possible in the back seat, unable to think of a single thing to say. We were each certain we had utterly failed as human beings.

The first time Lance "officially" took a girl out was no big deal. In fact, I'm not sure I remember it, or if he does. I think he took Connie James to a football game, and I vaguely recall him and Jason trying to persuade Mark to come along and drive for them. Mark, a year older, was the first to get his driver's license, but the last to get interested in girls.

By contrast, Laurie's first date is vividly etched in my mind. She spent two hours changing clothes, doing her hair, worrying that she looked awful and would say something stupid. She was certain the boy would hate her, tell his friends she was dull, and that she'd never be asked out again as long as she lived. Furthermore, if dating was going to be *that* much trouble, she didn't care (Laurie tends to be melodramatic).

We never set "official" dating rules for Lance. His guidelines came under the heading of common courtesy: pick up your date at her home, and have her back at least ten minutes before her curfew; let us know where and with whom you're going, and what time you will be home; if you are going to be even fifteen minutes late, *call*; and drive carefully.

The question of age came up with Laurie, since, generally, boys aren't interested in dating as early as girls are. Some parents set a specific number—fourteen, fifteen, sixteen. In our community most parents insist their children wait until high school, then allow them to date on a limited basis, mainly church and school events. We felt this was right and reasonable for Laurie.

Laurie must also ask *before* accepting a date with a boy we don't know, or for any unusual activity. She thinks this restriction is unnecessary, and also disagrees with our insistence that her dates pick her up at our house. I know times are different now, but I can't help thinking that a boy who is content to have his date meet him somewhere (except in special circumstances) isn't the kind we want Laurie to date.

A strict curfew doesn't seem to fit all situations, so we don't have one. If the ball game is over at 9:30, there's plenty of time to eat pizza and still be home by 11:00. If the party doesn't end until midnight, we don't insist Lance or Laurie leave early in order to meet a deadline. For both children, we feel dating should be restricted to weekends. Other times are best used for study, relaxing, or non-date school activities.

You know, Lord, that this business of dating has caused more parents more friction than any other single issue. Give us wisdom in setting guidelines. Don't let us be bound up in a set of rules that ignore people and circumstances. At the same time, help us to be firm in standing our ground when we know we're right. Let me, especially, remember that part of being a parent is being willing to be temporarily disliked. I must make unpopular decisions for my teens when they can't, or won't, make them for themselves.

Let Lance and Laurie realize, Lord, that with the increased freedom they desire comes increased responsibility. And as they demonstrate their growing maturity, let me be willing to turn over more and more decisions to them.

"Our greatest wish and prayer is that you will become mature Christians" (2 Cor. 13:9b).

I Want My Ring Back

"Susie called," I told Lance as he came in from work Saturday evening. "She wants you to call her back. Oh, and someone else called, too. She said her name was Kim something."

Lance's face brightened. "Kim Decker, I'll bet. I met her when I was delivering ice to the south IGA. Did she say what she wanted?"

"Huh-uh."

Lance went immediately to the telephone. His conversation with Susie was brief, but he visited quite awhile with Kim. Afterward he wandered back into the kitchen.

"Going out?" I asked.

He shook his head. Halfway embarrassed, he said, "I've got a real problem. I'd like to ask Kim out, but I can't as long as I'm going steady with Susie. I'd like my ring back, but I don't know how to get it."

The solution seemed obvious to me. "Ask for it! Tell Susie you think both of you would be happier if you weren't dating each other exclusively."

"I guess I'll have to," he said uncomfortably.

Lance looks so mature that I sometimes forget he's barely eighteen, socially inexperienced and unsure of himself. Rather than ask for the ring, he's spent the last several weeks dragging his feet. He's kept Susie, himself, and most likely this Kim in limbo. Surely Susie can read the signs! She's probably as ready as Lance to call it quits. After all, how much fun can it be to date a boy who hasn't taken her out in a month because: he's broke; he has to work late; he's going out with Jason and Mark; or (I never dreamed I'd hear this excuse!) he has to stay home and clean out the garage for his father.

So many young people have gotten more deeply into relationships than they ever intended because they didn't know how to make a clean break. They've drifted into going steady, engagement, even marriage without being precisely sure how it happened. Why? "We were comfortable together," one person says. "I didn't want to hurt his feelings," another explains. Others admit, "I wasn't sure I would ever find another boy/girl friend." Common attitudes, yes, but hardly the bases for lifelong commitment.

Please, dear Jesus, don't let Lance fall into these traps! Give him courage, and tact.

I hope he gets his ring back without hurting Susie's feelings. I hope he's able to date this Kim who has evidently captured his attention. Most especially, I hope he thinks twice before he gives his ring away again.

"Instead, we will lovingly follow the truth at all times— speaking truly, dealing truly, living truly. . ." (Eph. 4:15a).

Stood Up—Again

"That was Greg," Laurie said as she hung up the receiver. "He isn't coming." Her voice broke, and I held her in my arms while she cried. She's almost as tall as I, yet needs hugging as much as when she was two. Maybe more.

I feel so helpless! There's nothing, *nothing* I can do except hold her tight, and, for now, hold my tongue as well.

The last part isn't easy. This isn't the first date Greg has broken at the last minute, nor the second. I am filled with rage that he treats Laurie so inconsiderately! And I'm frustrated and puzzled that she lets him. Why doesn't she drop him and date the other boys who call?

Is this pain an inevitable part of growing up? I'm older than fifteen. Years older. But I remember. His name was Jim, and the hurt still lingers in the deep recesses of my mind.

Maybe I should use this memory to let Laurie know I understand. There are many Gregs (and Jims) in this world. They are undeniably charming. They know just what to say and how to act. They make a girl feel witty and wonderful and wanted.

Laurie must learn so many things. And she'll have to learn most of them, as I did, through experience. She'll find that superficial charm doesn't make up for lack of character; smooth talk can't hide selfishness—at least not for long; and feeling wonderful isn't the same as love. We've talked about these things, but at the moment Laurie is so "in like" with Greg she doesn't hear.

Father, Laurie has been hurt and disappointed. I'm sorry, but maybe it's not all bad. Maybe this experience will make her more careful of the feelings of others. Remind her, please, that words and actions she takes lightly might bitterly wound someone else.

Lord, I'm tempted to ask you to intervene and remove Greg from the scene; maybe he could move elsewhere, or find another girlfriend. In other words, I'm tempted to ask you to take responsibility that is mine. Forgive me for seeking an easy way out—for me and for Laurie.

When she's ready to talk, Lord, guide my words. Keep me from being super-critical or judgmental. But help me, please, to help Laurie see Greg as he is. Let her look through eyes that aren't blinded by infatuation.

"What counts is whether we really have been changed into new and different people" (Gal. 6:15b).

Nobody Asked Me

Beth and Kerri had mentioned the class Valentine party several times. When I asked Laurie about it, she said she wasn't going. The reason? Nobody had asked her.

"Is a date required?" I wondered. "Can't you go with other girls or by yourself?"

She rolled her eyes back in her head. "Go alone to a Sweetheart party? No thanks. It won't kill me to stay home."

From the tone of her voice, I knew it wasn't going to be much fun, either. Lance offered to fix her up, but all he got for his efforts was a dirty look. I suspect he deserved it. I've never met Hoss Harry or Clyde the Creep, but neither sounds like Laurie's type.

Laurie moped around until I'd had enough. "Does every boy you like have a date?" I asked.

She shrugged in that annoying "who cares" way she has, but I persisted. "You have plenty of friends who are boys. Why not invite one of them to go with you? There's no rule that says boys have to do all the asking."

Laurie acted shocked. "Me? Ask a guy? Never!"

But I noticed that the hopeless look left her face.

I used to think boys should always do the asking, except for those rare Sadie Hawkins type things. I also thought boys had it made since they got to ask, while girls had to sit around and wait. When I was Laurie's age and without a date, I usually assumed it was because I was dumb, ugly, fat, had a zero personality, or all those things put together.

My viewpoint took a sharp right turn when Lance began dating. Sure, boys get to ask. But they must also risk a refusal (sometimes rude or cutting), make all the plans, and pay for everything. Furthermore, just because a girl says yes is no guarantee a boy actually has a date; some girls "accept" several invitations, then cancel all but the best offer.

Shyness and fear keep a lot of boys from dating. For a long time Lance's friend Mark was so terrified at the prospect of asking a girl anything (even "What page is our history assignment?") that he didn't date at all. I've seen Lance pick up the telephone and put it down five times before summoning the courage to call a particular girl. And Jason confided that when he first started dating, he wrote out every word he intended to say and rehearsed in front of a mirror before confronting a potential date.

I suspect many boys would be secretly relieved if girls would occasionally take the initiative and call them—not all the time, not even most of the time. Maybe it's time things evened up a bit.

A girl shouldn't call a guy she's admired only from afar. She ought to make it clear what she has in mind, and who pays for what. But I see nothing wrong with a girl saying to a friend, "I have tickets to the concert Friday night. Would you like to go with me?"

If a girl isn't ready to ask a boy *out*, she could ask him *in*—into her home to make fudge, watch something special on television, or play Perquacky or Mastermind. Not only are home dates fun, but they take pressure off a guy's pocketbook. Lack of money keeps Lance and his friends dateless many Saturday nights.

This afternoon, Laurie came in from school all smiles. She was going to the party with Mike Moore. And *she'd* done the asking.

"It was the scariest moment of my life!" she said. "My hands were ice cold and my legs actually shook. But I did it anyway. I walked to the lockers with Mike after geometry, and mentioned that I didn't have a date for the party. Then I said that if he didn't either, maybe we could go together."

Bless Mike, Father, for responding so graciously, for telling Laurie he'd wanted to call, but assumed she'd be with Greg. Thank you that Mike promptly made the plans firm and asked her to dinner before the party. Thanks, too, for helping Laurie see that it's okay to reverse traditional roles. It took real courage for her to ask, and it's given her insight into what a boy goes through every time he wants a date.

Let them have an especially good time, Lord. I think they will. Whatever, there will be two less people sitting home alone, wishing they were together and joining the fun.

"Everything is appropriate in its own time. . ." (Eccles. 3:11a).

Two-O'Clock Call

I guess every mother has a horror of receiving a two-o'clock call. Whenever the telephone rings in the middle of the night, my heart jumps into my throat.

When the phone rang last night, I knew it was Lance. Laurie had been asleep for hours, and my husband had called earlier from his conference in Chicago. Lance was with some classmates at a basketball tournament in the city. He'd phoned about midnight to say he'd be late, but this was later than late.

"Where are you?" I practically shouted. "Are you all right?"

"I'm fine, but I'm still in the city. I hate to ask, but could you come get me? I guess the others aren't going to make it home."

"Where are you?"

"At that pizza place on Fifth and Meridian. It's about a block past the intersection of Highway 50 and Kingsdown Road. You've been there before."

I vaguely remembered it. "I'll be there as soon as I can," I told him.

I pulled on my jeans and coat, then pinned a note to Laurie's pillow in case she woke up (she never remembers anything I tell her when she's half-asleep). Nearly forty minutes passed before I pulled into the restaurant parking lot. It was deserted except for Lance, who was pacing back and forth on the sidewalk, trying to keep warm.

"How long have you been out in this weather?" I asked.

"Not long." He tried to reassure me. "They just closed a little while ago."

"Where are the others? What happened?"

"Like I said the first time I called, the tournament ran way late. But we were hungry and decided to eat before we started home. We came out here, and while we were eating some girls came in. We visited awhile; then someone suggested we hunt for an all-night spot instead of going home. When I couldn't change their minds, I checked to see if I could catch a late bus. There wasn't one, so I had to call you."

"I'm glad you did," I told him. I meant it. I'm glad he was willing to go against the crowd, glad he refused to participate in actions he felt were wrong.

I feel sorry for Lance, but not too sorry; part of this is his own fault. Since out-of-town trips are the norm in our travel-oriented community, we've stressed four guidelines for safety's sake: get prior approval from us; carry money for emergency gas, meals, or the telephone; if you need help or are uneasy about a situation, call immediately; and go only with people you know extremely well.

I'm thankful, Father, that Lance followed the first three. Next time, help him remember the fourth as well.

I think he will. The memory of a long wait in near-freezing temperatures will remain in his mind a long time. He'll have to work tomorrow after less than four hours' sleep, and that won't be pleasant either.

Thank you, Father, for keeping Lance safe. Let this experience be a valuable lesson. Don't let me grumble or complain about the trip or my interrupted sleep. Help me realize we learn through our mistakes.

And thank you that I didn't know Lance was waiting outside—alone—in the cold.

"So he returned home to his father. And while he was still a long distance away, his father saw him coming, and was filled with loving pity and ran and embraced him and kissed him" (Luke 15:20).

Her Parents Weren't Home

Jason was over this afternoon. When he told Lance and me about his Saturday night date, I was shocked. I shouldn't have been. From the advice given to young men in Proverbs, I guess the problem is age-old. Thinking back, I remembered a friend relating similar experiences when we were in college.

But I suspect many mothers are like me. We're used to the stereotype picture of man as the aggressor, woman as the pursued. We fail to prepare our sons for the time a girl will offer her body in a way that makes it difficult to refuse.

Jason met the girl over Cokes at the Hub. She called him that evening, and the next. Flattered, he asked her out. The night began as a normal Lance-or-Jason type date: they went to the movies, then ate tacos. When he took her home she invited him in—again, not unusual. Laurie's dates frequently come in for tea and cookies, especially if they're early or have been somewhere exciting. Lance brings dates by after a game or for an evening of television.

Only this girl's parents weren't home, and weren't going to be, and it would be wonderful if Jason could spend the night.

He didn't. He left her house fast. "She came on so strong I got scared," he admitted, laughing at himself. "At the same time it was embarrassing. All the way home I kept imagining her telling everyone in school that something was wrong with me, that I wasn't normal."

I could sympathize. In our society boys who don't engage in sex at every opportunity are sometimes made to feel they *are* abnormal. A guy who doesn't take whatever a girl offers (and push for more) is suspect. Very few voices speak up and tell the truth: that sex never made anyone a man; that not everybody is doing it (many fine young men respect God's commandments); and that those who give in to sexual temptation may find themselves with herpes, venereal disease, and even lifetime responsibility for an unwanted, unplanned child.

Thank you, Father, that Jason had the courage and presence of mind to leave immediately when he knew the situation wasn't right. Many times we flirt with temptation, enjoying the moment, until it's too late. Thank you for his positive self-image. Thank you, especially, for the wonderful sense of humor that lets him laugh at his own embarrassment.

Jason has thought of what he'll do if she calls again. Help him, Lord, to tell her about what you've done in his life. Touch her, and other teens like her. There are so many of them! They are desperate for love, but seeking it in the wrong places, in the wrong ways.

Give them your guidance, Lord. Lead them to the real, true love that we find only in you.

"Let your manhood be a blessing. . ." (Prov. 5:18a).

Eight of Us

Laurie, dateless on a Saturday night, was going skating with four of her friends. She'd been slightly despondent when she left, so I was surprised when she came home bubbling over.

"Guess who showed up at the skating rink? Lance and Jason and Mark! They skated with us; then all eight of us went for pizza. It was really a fun evening."

I was even more surprised when Lance agreed. It was the best Saturday night he'd had since the last time a group got together informally.

I think this is the way the Lord meant for boys and girls to get to know each other—in groups. There is no pressure to pair off or become intimate. The quieter teen needn't worry about being a sparkling conversationalist; with seven other kids along, a listener is appreciated. There's less worry about money when each person pays his own share. (Lance says it takes at least $20 to treat a girl to a movie and a decent dinner.)

Groups can get a bad name, I know. Certainly, some groups exert pressure to conform, and occasionally a group turns into a mob. But a group of Christian kids can't be beat, and I'm thankful that Lance and Laurie have discovered the fun they can have as part of a group like tonight's.

Help me, Lord, to encourage group activities. Lance and Laurie already feel comfortable bringing their friends here. Let me continue to make their guests feel welcome. (It's easier for me than for some mothers, Lord. I genuinely enjoy their friends, and I'm not bothered by a too-loud record player, a wastebasket overflowing with pop cans, or even four sleeping bags spread out on Laurie's floor.) Maybe I could go a step further, though. We could have a cookout, or an afternoon of touch football, or games and popcorn and candied apples.

Thank you that our church realizes the importance of boy-girl activities. The youth group recently has had a hayride, an afternoon of bowling, and a Saturday lake party. The annual New Year's Eve get-together takes pressure to have a date off many kids, since singles, couples, and even groups of eight are welcome and can have fun.

Thank you that everyone had a good time tonight. Help them remember the fun, and to go as a group again soon.

"But if we are living in the light of God's presence, just as Christ does, then we have wonderful fellowship and joy with each other. . ." (1 John 1:7).

5

School Days

The Teacher Hates Me

"She did it again!" Laurie shouted as she stormed in from school.

"Who did what?" I asked, although I was afraid I knew the answer.

"Mrs. Kincaid, the old bat! Who else?" Laurie poured herself a glass of milk and drank half of it. "I walked into class just as the bell rang. She marked me late for not being in my seat and gave me two demerits!"

"Pretty stiff," I agreed. "You'd better make sure you're early after this."

"Mom, she hates me! Three football jocks strolled in while she was bawling me out, and she didn't give them any demerits or even scold them! And look at this!"

Laurie handed me her report on the Lincoln-Douglas debates. She'd spent a day in the library doing research, and had skipped a Saturday bike trip to write it. On the report cover was a big red "C" and a terse note: "You are capable but lazy."

Laurie was close to tears. "This is every bit as good as Beth's report, and she got an 'A'! I might as well have handed in blank pages. Nothing I do pleases Mrs. Kincaid."

School is such an important part of a teenager's life. When there is trouble with one teacher, the whole day goes sour. While grades aren't all-important, several of Laurie's activities depend on high marks: National Honor Society, Student Council, even future college scholarships. It's not right for these to be jeopardized unfairly.

I'm tempted to call the school principal and voice a loud complaint. Yet I hesitate, knowing quarrels are rarely one-sided. I vividly remember the time Lance received a "D" in science, his best subject.

He was furious. "I aced the six-week test!" he claimed. "My experiments were tops in the class! The teacher cheated me out of an 'A'!"

I would have rushed (vigorously) to Lance's defense. Fortunately, my husband's voice of reason prevailed. "Lance should make an appointment with the teacher," he said. "Hopefully this matter can be resolved between the two of them."

It was, and the science teacher became one of Lance's favorite instructors. You see, Lance had indeed "aced" his tests. His experiments *were* tops. But he hadn't bothered to hand in his "boring" daily assignments—and didn't tell us that part.

Lance and Laurie have had a few minor problems with teachers. We've encouraged them to work things out themselves. Laurie's problem with a coach was based on misunderstanding, and quickly cleared up when she went to practice half an hour early and talked with him. Lance has had to accept the fact that his physics teacher is extremely demanding, and now spends the extra hours of study needed to make a good grade.

Some school situations, though, require adult intervention. Lance had a first-grade teacher who actually locked children in a dark supply closet if they misbehaved. (She was found to have severe emotional problems and was released.) Another teacher once flew at Jason in a rage, scratching at his face until she brought blood. At times like these, a visit to the principal or even the school board is certainly in order.

Laurie's trouble falls in between the two extremes. There are so many questions, and no pat answers! Does Laurie need help, or should she just tough it out? Perhaps she needs to examine her behavior; it's possible she's doing something to irritate her teacher. It's possible, too, that Mrs. Kincaid has outside problems that affect her relationship with Laurie.

Be with her, Lord, and guide her in both school and home life.

Remind me to pray (and count to ten or even a thousand) before placing blame or springing blindly to my child's defense. On the other hand, don't let me be reluctant to interfere in *any* student's behalf when there is a real need.

Above all, give me the wisdom to know when to act, and when to let you act.

"We can always 'prove' that we are right, but is the Lord convinced? Commit your work to the Lord, then it will succeed" (Prov. 16:2, 3).

Too Much to Do

"How was school?" I asked Laurie.

"Fine," she answered, and immediately burst into tears.

The problem is common—too many things to do and not enough time to do them. Tonight is the season's first football game; Laurie must be at the stadium early to pass out "Go Lions" buttons. She spent an hour after school decorating for the after-game party, and must stay to clean up when it's over. Two teachers made assignments to be completed over the weekend, but when? Tomorrow Laurie has to work at the cheerleader Bake Sale from 9:00 until 2:00, and the church youth group has tickets for a concert tomorrow night. Between Sunday school, worship, and youth group, there aren't many spare hours on Sunday, either.

Whoever started the rumor (and why has it persisted!) that the teen years are always fun-filled and carefree? My own high school days were so hectic I developed a nervous twitch in my face and sometimes fell asleep in class. One of my friends actually had a complete emotional breakdown. And I honestly believe it's worse today. Sometimes it seems like kids are supposed to do and be all things—perfectly!

Lord, help Laurie slow down. Give her wisdom in choosing her activities. Guide her priorities, gently reminding her that you are supposed to have first place. Thank you for the decisions she's made: she didn't try out for drill team, even though Beth and Kerri begged her to join; she refused an office in Kayettes, knowing she wouldn't have time to do a good job. Show her, please, if she needs to drop additional activities. Keep her from putting pressure on herself, and help her resist pressure from others, including me.

Let me help Laurie, too. I can remember that most teens need extra sleep. Next Saturday, when there's nothing going on (I hope!), I'll let her sleep all morning. I can make sure she eats right, and supplement her diet with vitamins if needed. During busy times like this, I can be especially patient and understanding.

Please, Lord, see Laurie through this frantically paced weekend. If her strength fails, lend her yours. And help her remember the football cheers—all thirty-eight of them!

"Teach us to number our days and recognize how few they are; help us to spend them as we should" (Ps. 90:12).

I Blew It!

"How did you do?" I asked when Lance returned from the High School Bowl competition.

"I blew it!" he said, his voice full of disgust. "We lost, and it was all my fault."

"Lance, there are three others on the team. There's no way you could be the only one responsible for losing."

"Oh, no? Just ask my teammates. There was a minute to go in the championship match with Lincoln, and we were tied. So, idiot me, I did the one thing Mr. Ryden told us not to do: I pressed the buzzer before the moderator finished reading the question."

"And you didn't know the answer?"

Lance made a face. "The answer was right, but the question wasn't. I thought he wanted O. Henry's real name, which is William Sydney Porter. I was supposed to name one of the short stories that made him famous."

" 'The Ransom of Red Chief' or 'The Gift of the Magi'," I said automatically.

"Lincoln knew them too, so they won. Mr. Ryden is furious. I really blew it."

"I blew it." How often I have come before God and said those very words! Is there anyone who hasn't experienced that sick, sinking sensation that comes when he's goofed? We can apologize until we're blue, but nothing can undo the damage.

Sometimes I think I've blown it with Lance and Laurie more than my share of times. I remember particularly the Christmas Laurie was twelve. She was going to sing "What Child Is This?" for morning worship—her first solo. I promised to lower the music three steps, but when I sat down at the piano I forgot. Laurie's voice grew thin and finally cracked as she strained to reach notes that were too high.

As soon as we reached the car she began sobbing wildly. "I've never been so humiliated in all my life! I was awful! I'll never sing again!"

But three hours later (after two dear ladies in our congregation called to compliment her lovely voice) Laurie hugged me, assuring me everything was fine again and maybe her life wasn't ruined after all. Last year, remembering the incident, she said it had actually helped! Having lived through that, she could handle anything that happened while she sang.

Just last year I carelessly tossed Lance's track jersey into a washer that contained something red. I bleached and bleached, but during every meet at least one person referred to him as "the kid in pink." And when Lance was a freshman I threw away (and burned) nine weeks' worth of biology notes—two days before semester tests.

I've blown it in other ways, too. I've given sympathy when I should have stood tough, and made demands when I needed to provide comfort. I've been too lenient in some things, too strict in others.

Thank you, Father, that they are growing in your grace in spite of my mistakes.

Right now, nothing I say or do will lessen Lance's disappointment in himself and his performance. Only time will heal the hurt and erase the memory. Even though he blew it, help him to learn from this and give him courage to try again, and again, and again.

And, Lord, let Mr. Ryden be as ready to forgive Lance as Lance and Laurie are to forgive me—and as you are to forgive all of your children.

"A man who rerfuses to admit his mistakes can never be successful. But if he confesses and forsakes them, he gets another chance" (Prov. 28:13).

Male Chauvinist Piglet

Lance and Laurie are supporting different candidates for student body president.

"The only qualification Brice Jacobs has is his football reputation," Laurie said of Lance's preference. "He's never been a class officer. And he barely has a 'C' average."

"So?" Lance countered in that insolent tone he knows makes Laurie furious.

"So Tina Mitchell has a 3.87 grade average in the Honors program. She has specific proposals for improving the school. She's held several class offices and last year was student body secretary."

"If she were running for secretary again, I'd vote for her," Lance said. "But the president ought to be a *guy*."

"Why?" Laurie and I asked simultaneously.

"Because boys make better leaders."

"You know what you are, Lance?" Laurie asked coldly. "A male chauvinist pig, that's what." She stared at him a moment. "No, I take that back. You're not big enough to be a pig. You're a male chauvinist *piglet*!"

At the moment, I agree with her. I'm angry at Lance's attitude, and disturbed because so many of his friends seem to share it. Too often I hear comments such as "What do you expect from a girl?" or "That's just like a female."

Are they really putting women down? Or am I too sensitive about this issue of equality? Maybe—I certainly hope so—this is simply a natural part of growing up—a phase.

To be fair, most of today's young men hold ideas that are far different from those common a generation ago. Lance supports equal pay for equal (or comparable) work, the right to participate freely in government, the right to the same educational and job opportunities. On an individual basis I think he views and treats girls as equals: Kim is just as bright as he, Tina much brighter; Laurie is a better basketball player; Mari's quarter-mile track time is good for anyone, male or female.

Maybe I'd better examine my own attitudes, Lord. Have I viewed women as somehow weaker or inferior? Or, conversely, been strident and militant, claiming superiority? If so, forgive me. Help our family to be a living lesson in equality of opportunity, dignity, and service.

Keep Lance's attitudes flexible, Lord. Help him to reject stereotypes and prejudicial labels. Help him to become secure enough in himself that he needn't build self-esteem by trampling on another's dignity.

In the school elections, I surely hope the best qualified candidate wins. Don't you?

"We are no longer . . . even merely men and women, but we are all the same—we are Christians; we are one in Christ Jesus" (Gal. 3:28).

Tryouts

Laurie is trying out for varsity cheerleader this afternoon. She and Beth and Kerri have been practicing their routines for weeks—new ones like "Funky Chicken" and "Whoop-te-doo," oldies like "We've Got the Team." At the moment, Laurie's whole future hinges on being one of the eight girls selected.

At the same time, she's concerned about Kerri. "You know what her mother told her?" she asked. Her voice shook with indignation. "She said if Kerri didn't get cheerleader, it would break the family tradition. Even her grandmother was one!"

"Tell her I wasn't," I said to Laurie. It won't help, and Laurie won't tell. But maybe it will ease Laurie's mind to know that neither my love nor our family pride is at stake this afternoon.

Why do some parents put such pressure on their children? Why do they see their children's achievements (and failures) as reflections on themselves? Please, Lord, help Kerri deal with this pressure. Help her mother take pride in Kerri's many music awards and straight "A" scholarship. Keep her from demanding a carbon copy of herself, and let her assure Kerri of her continuing love.

Maybe it's easier for me, Lord. As a teen I was often a "failure." Yet looking back from the vantage point of twenty-odd years, I realize my failures taught me more than my successes. I wasn't the smartest, so I learned to study. I wasn't the prettiest, so I developed conversational abilities. I was a poor athlete, but I found two solitary sports I enjoyed—walking and swimming—and I still enjoy them today. I certainly wasn't the most popular, so I had time alone to discover and develop me.

There are times when I want more than Lance or Laurie can give, even if it's only at that moment. *Stop me*, please, when I ask too much. Help me, help all parents, find the right balance in our expectations. We don't want to demand so little our children do nothing, or so much they break under the pressure.

Give us wisdom to keep our demands in line with yours. You are concerned with lives lived in obedience to your will, whatever activities, achievements, awards and disappointments our children experience along the way.

Lord, this is a big day for the girls who are trying out for cheerleader. Bless them, help each and every one to do her best.

Win or lose, give Laurie, give all the girls, grace and dignity to cope.

"Don't keep on scolding and nagging your children, making them angry and resentful. Rather, bring them up with the loving discipline the Lord himself approves, with suggestions and godly advice" (Eph. 6:4).

They Lost Again

They lost. This was the sixteenth loss in a row, the longest losing streak of any girls' basketball team in the school's history. I ached for Laurie as she walked off the court, her head bowed and shoulders slumped. She was the picture of defeat.

The game was so close! Right up until the final buzzer, I

hoped (prayed, really) they might pull it off. I know Laurie blames herself for missing the last-second shot.

Different people handle defeat in different ways. Lance has always had a firm sense of his own worth; losing doesn't alter it. When he's been beaten in a race, he asks himself "Why?" If he was slow out of the starting blocks or misjudged an opponent, he works to correct the problem. If the winner was simply a faster runner, he accepts the fact. He loves to win, but I don't think the medals and ribbons really matter; they're hidden away in his bottom drawer.

To Laurie, a loss is temporarily devastating. She needs time alone to cry, to hurt, to recover. When she's ready to talk about the game she will. I've learned not to say those things that spring so quickly to a parent's mind and lips: "You played so well. . . . It's only a game. . . . Next time you'll do better."

Laurie isn't staying down nearly as long this year, and a lot of the credit for that goes to our new coach. He's helped her set goals for each game and for the season. He tells her, "You win when you better your performance and strive to reach your personal goals."

The goals aren't what I might have expected: score so many points or grab so many rebounds. Her season goals are these: to play aggressively but under control (the aggression is easy, the control is not!); to improve her defensive play; to shoot whenever she is open; and to keep her temper when the referee makes a poor call or she makes a mistake.

The coach also had her set character-improvement goals. At first I thought it was silly, but I'm beginning to see that Laurie approaches life in much the same manner as she plays ball—aggressively, but not always under control. She's now striving to keep her emotions on a more even keel, and do what is right even though she doesn't feel like it.

Thank you, Lord, that she is learning to depend on you

for strength and guidance. Thank you, too, for this young coach who is so patient with Laurie.

Win or lose, Lord, I enjoy watching Laurie play ball. She's so at ease with her body! Surely that grace is a gift from you! But Laurie isn't thinking about that now, Lord. Her mind is filled with this loss. Comfort her, please. Help her cope with this defeat, learn from it, and grow stronger.

And Lord, please, let them win. Just once.

"To win the contest you must deny yourselves many things that would keep you from doing your best" (1 Cor. 9:25a).

Benchwarmer

Again tonight I'm watching Laurie's team play basketball. I love seeing her on the court. At the same time, my heart goes out to the girls who sit on the bench.

They practice two or more hours each day. They observe the training rules. They watch every game, they cheer, they hope—hope for the opportunity to play. I can see the longing in their eyes. I've even seen lips moving in prayer: "Please, Lord, let me go in."

There are a few super-athletes, I'm sure, who are so talented they skip the apprenticeship of waiting and giving way to older, more experienced players. Most players, though, must serve their time as "subs." Lance watched and hoped through several sports until he discovered he could run well. Laurie spent much of each game on the bench in early junior high; it's only now she seems to be coming into her own.

Sports is big business. I read in a national magazine that pressure to perform and win has actually driven some budding young athletes to suicide. Others seek to escape through drugs or alcohol. Most of the time (not all, just most) I'm grateful that neither Lance nor Laurie is exceptionally talented. It makes it easier for all of us to keep high school sports in the proper perspective. Being a star has little bearing on success in life. The important things are having fun, keeping fit, and playing fairly.

Everytime I come to a game I think of Lance's friend Denny, who graduated last year. He made the varsity team two years, and spent most of those years on the bench. It wasn't lack of effort; if practice and desire were the only factors, Denny would have made All-State. Yet he never complained, but encouraged other players, and kept his sense of humor.

"You can tell the score by looking at me," he once joked. "If I'm in the game, we're twenty points ahead or behind."

Why did he stay on the team? "I love basketball," he explained. "I'm not tall or talented, but I enjoy playing, even in practice."

At Awards Night, Denny received the Coach's Trophy for "Most Dedicated Athlete," plus a standing ovation from us all.

Lord, give everyone on the bench that selfless spirit. Let this be a time of learning and growing. Help them realize they are an important part of the team. Make sure Laurie and the other starters recognize and appreciate their contributions.

I want to add a prayer right now. We're sixteen points down with only three minutes left to play. Please, move Coach to send these girls into the game. I know how important it is. Once I was a benchwarmer, too.

"And some of the parts that seem weakest and least important are really the most necessary" (1 Cor. 12:22).

A Tenth of a Second

Yesterday Lance ran in the regional track meet. He's done very well this year, surprising his coach, us, and even himself. He won the 400-meter dash at three different meets, and anchored the relay team that posted the state's third best time in our class. A week ago he received a letter from the track coach at State University: "We'll watch for you at the state meet . . . we are interested. . . ."

"Purple and white, here I come!" Lance said. He was joking, but I could tell he was beginning to dream of big-time athletics.

The trouble with dreams is waking up. The relay team had a bad baton exchange between the second and third runners. They ended up five seconds off their pace and were eliminated by teams they'd previously defeated.

The top three 400-meter runners would win the right to compete in the state meet. Two athletes had posted better times than Lance, so he'd need to run his best. I know a race shouldn't be so important, but I was almost praying when Lance went to the blocks. He got a good start and ran a strong race, but was nipped for third as they crossed the finish line.

I batted back tears of disappointment as Lance, his sides heaving from the exertion, shook hands with those who had defeated him. I was grateful for the grace, or habit, that helped him be a gracious-appearing loser.

I wanted to run to him, throw my arms around him and console him as I'd done when he was tiny. I longed to, but of course I didn't. I sat in the stands with a smile pasted on my face, applauding mechanically as the winner of each race broke the tape. In my mind I was replaying Lance's races, the "if-onlys" eating at me like a cancer.

After twenty minutes Lance came up and sat beside me. "You ran really well," I told him.

To my surprise he nodded. "I had my best time ever. It just wasn't fast enough. I missed third by one tenth of a second." He laughed, but it had a forced, hollow sound. "Purple and white, there I went."

This morning, when I was vacuuming his room, the letter from State was crumpled into a tight ball, lying on the floor.

It isn't easy to lose, Lord. It's even harder not to make excuses for your losses. Thank you that Lance had the maturity not to blame his failure to qualify on track conditions, poor coaching, or even sore feet. I heard all those excuses and more from people sitting around me.

Thank you that running is not Lance's whole life, that he has other interests and is secure enough about himself that this loss can be taken in stride. Help him to be realistic about his abilities, but not so easily discouraged that he gives up on a dream. He may not be fast enough to run for State, but there are other schools.

I'll add a prayer, Lord, for all athletes—those who finish first and those who finish last. If they have fun competing, if they learn something, if they meet new people and make new friends, then surely they are all winners.

Oh, before I say "amen," I need to pray for me. Keep me from the temptation to be disappointed when my children's performances are less than perfect. Don't let me be a stage mama, living out my fantasies through Lance and Laurie. Let me keep sports and grades and honors where they belong, remembering that the "good race" is not an earthly one.

"An athlete goes to all this trouble just to win a blue ribbon or a silver cup, but we do it for a heavenly reward that never disappears" (1 Cor. 9:25b).

Graduation Day

This has been a hectic day. We have a houseful of company. There was a mix-up on the cakes for the reception, and I spent an hour on the telephone trying to straighten it out. It took another half hour to press Lance's robe—the wrinkles didn't "hang out" like the label said they would.

We had an early, rushed supper, the dishwasher broke, and the car wouldn't start.

Now, finally, everything is under control. The caterer delivered the cakes and the reception area looks marvelous. Lance will be wrinkle-free as he walks in with his class. My mother and sister (bless them!) washed all the dishes, and my husband's minor surgery on the car was successful.

At the opening strains of the processional, we stand to honor the graduates. Lance tries to look serious, but I catch the twinkle in his eye. He isn't sad to be leaving high school. It was fun, but he's looking forward to the next stage of life.

I can't concentrate on the speakers. I keep thinking, instead, of the changes his graduation will make in our lives. Can I remember to cook only half as much? Will we miss the track meets and programs and noisy friends? Laurie will have the biggest adjustment, I believe. Last summer Lance was away for two weeks. Laurie declared it great to be free of bossy old Lance! And it was great—for four whole days. When he returned she had tears of joy in her eyes as she hugged him.

Thank you, Lord, for the friends and relatives who have come to share our joy tonight, for my mother and sister, my husband's parents. Jon and Kiki and their folks are across the aisle, and Beth's family is behind us. It's good to know they care.

Bless those who are absent—the dear ones whose age and health wouldn't permit the trip, and my brother who lives halfway across the country. I know they are with us in spirit.

Thank you for the cards and gifts Lance has received, some of them wonderful surprises! There's a portable cassette recorder from his current best girl, a pile of lovely shirts and sweaters, a fishing rod and reel from a former employer, even a cap with his name on it from one of the boys who ran with him. Lance ordered two boxes of thank-you notes. I hope he is prompt in using them!

The speakers are finished. The young men and women are now parading across the stage to receive their diplomas. As Lance moves the tassle on his cap, memories come flooding into my mind. There was the time he and his dog ran away; the afternoon he amused himself by punching holes in each of his grandmother's lipsticks (she thought he was taking a nap!); the year he was the world's skinniest Santa in the class play.

Lance and Mark and Jason have had so many good times, Lord. Be with each of them as they go to different schools, different lives. I remember triumphs and tragedies, laughter and tears. It's odd (and perhaps kind) that time has a way of making them all seem less important.

The ceremony has ended. We stand once more as the graduates march past. Around me I hear some muffled sobs, but I feel no urge to cry. Lance is happy and so am I. He looks my way and grins. As he turns, his tassle swings into his mouth. We struggle to hold back our shared laughter.

Thank you, Lord, from the bottom of my heart that this young man is my child—and yours.

"Children are a gift from God; they are his reward" (Ps. 127:3).

6

Mirror, Mirror, on the Wall

Fat Attack

"I'm not eating tonight," Laurie announced, taking only three plates from the cabinet. "I've got to lose some weight."

"Why?" Lance deadpanned. "We don't care if you look like Miss Piggy's twin. We're your family, and we like you fat."

Instead of her usual snappy retort, Laurie burst into tears and fled into her room.

The rest of us had finished dinner before I found out what started it all. She had been measured for her cheerleader uniform after school. Laurie had to order a size seven, while the other girls could fit into fives and even threes.

"Laurie, you're at least two inches taller than any of them!" I reminded her. "You need a larger size for length as much as anything. And a seven is hardly a matronly size!"

"I know," she admitted. "But when I was standing there, the biggest girl in the room, all of a sudden I felt fat and disgusting! I really hated how I looked! Then tonight Lance said I was as fat as Miss Piggy—and I guess I overreacted." She laughed, but quickly became serious again. "Mom, *promise* you'll tell me if I start to get even a little bit fat. Okay?"

"Laurie, I promise."

My sister once gave me an apron that has "No woman can ever be too rich or too thin" printed on the front. In our society, at least, it's true. Although Laurie could carry another ten pounds without being even slightly plump, and her hyperactive personality further reduces the chance of being heavy, she still suffers attacks of "fat anxiety." So do I. I'm the right weight for my height, but I sometimes feel lumpish and ugly compared with the hollow-cheeked mannequins in fashion magazines.

Increasingly, the problem of "fat" gets out of hand. A girl in Lance's class was hospitalized last month with anorexia nervosa, a disorder practically unheard of ten years ago. She had been literally starving herself to death in an attempt to be acceptably thin. Laurie has a friend who forces herself to vomit after every meal; the girl thinks it's the only way she can keep from gaining weight. Last night's newspaper carried the story of a girl who tried to kill herself because she was too short and muscular to be "pretty."

Wouldn't it be wonderful if we could accept the fact that women come in a variety of shapes and sizes, and all of them can be attractive? There are some positive signs. A growing number of women are revolting against "thin is in" stereotyping. One of Laurie's magazines uses only models who appear well-nourished and healthy. The editors have also printed a couple of articles aimed at helping girls achieve a positive body image—to accept and *like* themselves as they are.

Thank you, Lord, for these steps, however small, in the right direction. Thank you, too, that Laurie is interested in keeping her body active, attractive, healthy, and yes, slim—real obesity is a health hazard and a social handicap. But don't let her get hung up on "fat"! Help her realize that a beautiful body won't last, but a beautiful spirit will be hers for all eternity.

For our whole family's health, let me run our kitchen

with an eye to proper nutrition. I can keep fresh fruits and vegetables available (and in sight!) and stop buying and making sugar-laden sweets. I can also remember not to make food an issue; a missed meal, like Laurie's dinner tonight, will not injure her one bit.

Let Laurie—let all girls—view themselves with the same appreciative enthusiasm they did when they were three. "We're lovely!" Laurie and Beth used to tell me.

They were, and they are. We're all beautiful, Lord, because we are made in your image.

"Be beautiful inside, in your hearts, with the lasting charm of a gentle and quiet spirit which is so precious to God" (1 Pet. 3:4.)

Where's the Clearasil?

The proofs for Lance's senior pictures came today, and I'm delighted with the way they turned out. In my favorite pose, Lance is standing beneath a tree, his suit coat thrown casually over his shoulder. He's smiling, and for once there's no glare on his glasses. Most important, the spots on his face don't show at all.

The day of the photographer's sitting began with Lance bellowing, "Where's the Clearasil? We're not out, are we?"

We were, and he had to make do with some perfumy blemish medicine of Laurie's. He left in a huff, and I was afraid the pictures would reflect his mood—not to mention the spots.

In a way, though, I'm glad for that morning. It reminded me that boys as well as girls care about their looks. Jason, for instance, worries because he's short and his shoulders are bony. Mark thinks his slightly hooked nose makes him look like a vulture. One of their classmates has complexion problems that make Lance's occasional spots seem insignificant; twice a month the boy must have infected cysts lanced and drained by a physician.

Still, looks (or lack of them) don't seem to affect a boy's standing or popularity in the same way they do a girl's. Intelligence, personality, and athletic ability seem to have far more influence than looks. The president of the Student Council walks with a pronounced limp. This year's Sweetheart King has a fat face and buck teeth.

A girl with comparable looks would have to forget about being Homecoming Queen. It's not likely she'd be selected cheerleader, or even chosen to perform in the Lionettes, the school's precision drill team.

There's a double standard, Lord, and it's not fair.

Still, I realize I'm seeing things from a woman's point of view. Help me remember that boys, too, really care how they look. Reassure those who feel deficient or inadequate because of some "abnormal" physical attribute.

Remind me, Lord, that while acne seems minor to parents, it's a mountainous problem to affected teens. Recently, 2,000 teens were asked, "What do you most dislike about yourself?" The answer most often given (by a wide margin) was, "My skin. It keeps breaking out."

We adults are looking back, Lord. We know that pimples don't last forever. Teens, though, have neither our years nor our smooth complexions. Don't let us treat this problem lightly. Let us encourage good home care, but be willing to consult a dermatologist if that doesn't do the job.

Above all, let me be understanding when Lance's face breaks out. And thank you, from both of us, that his spots didn't show up in the picture.

"It is a wonderful thing to be alive!" (Eccles. 11:7).

Someone Ought to Tell Him

Lance and Mark came in from school holding their noses and making gagging sounds.

"Some strange disease?" I asked.

Mark nodded. "This guy in our physics class smells so bad we nearly get sick. Even the teacher noticed! It was freezing outdoors, but he opened a window anyway."

"Maybe it isn't as easy for this boy to keep clean as it is for you two," I suggested. "Remember that friend of yours, Lance, whose family lived in a van?"

"This kid isn't deprived, not by a long shot," Mark said. "It's Chuck Barnett from the Crown Heights addition."

"Maybe he has some sort of physical problem," I said.

"He's dirty," Lance said flatly. "Plain old dirty. His clothes have food spots on them and he smells like he hasn't showered in a month. It's awful, and someone ought to tell him so."

I agreed. "Is there a teacher who could do it tactfully?"

They thought a minute. "Maybe Coach," Mark said. "We'll ask him. If he won't, maybe one of us could catch Chuck privately."

I opened my mouth to speak, but I didn't need to.

"I know what you're going to say," Lance told me. "Don't worry. Mark and I will do our very best not to hurt Chuck's feelings."

They grabbed a dozen cookies and headed for Lance's room to study.

I know God wants us to have clean hearts and minds. But physical cleanliness is important, too, if only out of consideration for those around us. What is the problem with Chuck? Ignorance? Laziness? Bombarded as we are with ads for soaps, deodorants, mouthwash, and the like, it's hard to imagine that anyone could be unaware of the basics of good personal hygiene. Does the boy have an emotional problem? Psychiatrists say disregard of one's personal appearance is one of the first signs of acute depression.

Sometimes we parents get so busy we forget our children don't automatically know how to care for their new, adult bodies. Lance was fortunate that his first coach, back in seventh grade, had a "man-to-man" talk with the athletes about cleanliness. I remember laughing to myself when Lance brought home the list of things he needed for track; along with running shoes and gym shorts were "soap, shampoo, and deodorant." Looking back, though, I'm grateful for the coach's concern. He no doubt spared several boys from potential embarrassing problems.

Certainly, Lord, it's not easy for everyone to be clean. Even in this privileged country there are those who don't have the laundering and bathing facilities I take for granted. Don't let me ever look down on them. Instead, may I freely share my resources so that their condition may be improved.

On the other hand, don't let embarrassment keep me (or Lance or Mark) from speaking frankly but gently to someone like Chuck.

It could be he simply needs to know—or needs to know that someone cares.

"Create in me a new, clean heart, O God, filled with clean thoughts and right desires" (Ps. 51:10).

A Real Three-Bagger

My nephew Matt was visiting, and Lance had promised to get him a date for Saturday night's party. With that in mind, the boys were lying on the living room floor poring over the pictures in Lance's yearbook. I couldn't help but overhear the conversation, and I didn't like it! The talk went like this:

Matt (after a preliminary scan of the photos): "You sure have a lot of ugly girls in your school. Something in the water?"

Lance (after an appreciative laugh): "Could be. There are some cute girls, though. You just have to hunt to find them."

Matt: "Is this one a girl or a boy?"

Lance: "A girl, you dope. How many boys do you know named Marilyn? She throws shot for the girls' track team. Her arms are as big as my legs."

Matt: "What about this one? Jenna."

Lance: "She's cute. About 5'3", blond hair, really nice figure. She's taken, though. Jason's cousin is dating her."

Matt: "What's this? An elephant?"

Lance: "Man, talk about three-baggers. She's the ugliest girl in the school."

Matt: "Maybe in the state." (Silence.) "This one's kind of pretty."

Lance: "The picture makes her look better than she is. She dresses funny and has toothpicks for legs."

Matt: "I'll pass, then." (More silence.) "Hey, what about Kay Kimball? She looks neat—and I think I met her up here last year."

Lance: "I thought you might remember her. She's cute and a lot of fun. I'll call her for you."

I was really disappointed in the boys' sense of values! Not once did either of them mention the important matters: "Is she a Christian? What are her interests? Do you think we'd have a good time together?" Not once! The way they discussed those girls made me think of a locker plant I visited—rows and rows of carcasses hanging there waiting to be inspected and stamped. "Choice" all the way down to "poor."

I told them what I thought, of course. Lance's response was to give me a look of sheer bewilderment.

"We're not being cruel. It's just that Matt doesn't want to get stuck with a dog! No guy does!"

I consoled myself by remembering that the girls Lance dates aren't all beauties. Kim isn't, although when she smiles she's radiant. I know, too, that Lance has been really disappointed in some beautiful girls. After a first and last date with one who could rival Brooke Shields, he commented, "She sure proved the old saying that beauty is skin deep, but ugly goes clear to the bone!"

Still, pretty girls are asked out first, and more often. Many girls with much to offer in the way of talent, character, and personality sit home simply because they don't meet current standards of beauty.

It isn't fair, Lord. It makes me angry that Lance and his friends place so much emphasis on the way a girl looks. Help them to see girls through *your* eyes. Let them look beyond the superficial trappings and discover the unique inner beauty you have given to each person. If there's something I can do to influence their attitudes, let me do it. So far, I've made little impression.

Be with the girls Lance and Matt discussed and rejected, Lord. Don't let them be hurt by others' attitudes. If they need help with grooming or weight control or hair styling, help them get it. And please, keep them from discouragement. Assure them of their worth in your sight.

Forgive Lance and Matt for their uncaring attitudes. As they grow in you, let them grow in grace toward others.

"Men judge by outward appearance, but I look at a man's thoughts and intentions" (1 Sam. 16:7b).

Jackie's Home!

"That was Jackie!" Laurie said excitedly as she hung up the telephone. "She's home, and the doctor says she can come to school Monday."

"Wonderful! How is she feeling?"

"Pretty good, physically. Emotionally she's having a rough time, and she's terrified of going back to classes. She's convinced she's so disfigured everyone will stare, and no guy will ever ask her out again."

"Can you help?"

Laurie nodded. "Beth and I are spending Sunday night

with her so we can help get her ready. Her balance is still off, and she can't completely dress herself. She can do her make-up fairly well, but she's really worried about her hair. She said the way her mom's fixed the wig makes her look like a clown." Laurie thought a moment. "Would you mind if I gave Jackie the slacks and blouse you brought me from Dallas? I was saving them for the Valentine party, but that color would be perfect for Jackie. Besides, she's lost so much weight nothing she has fits right."

My first thought was of the cost. I doubt that there will be money for another "special" outfit for Laurie. My second thought, though, was to silently praise the Lord for Laurie's willingness to help a friend.

"That's a lovely idea, Laurie," I said.

With that, she went to get the clothing and to consult with Beth.

Jackie and her parents have endured a heartbreaking crisis. The doctors believe the radical surgery plus chemotherapy have halted the spread of the cancer. One specialist even used (although cautiously) the word "cured." The therapist spoke of a "perfectly normal life."

Only it's not normal to have just one arm. Or no hair. This terrible disease has robbed Jackie of so much more than these physical things. It's taken her image of herself as an attractive, normal girl and replaced it with the picture of a person who is maimed and worthless and ugly. She thinks she'll never be pretty or desirable again. At fifteen, that feeling is almost too much to bear.

Lord, please make your abiding presence known to Jackie and all handicapped teenagers. If restoration of their bodies isn't possible in this life, renew their spirits! Let them find wholeness and worth in you.

Be with Laurie and Beth as they go to help Jackie. Thank you that their concern goes beyond a hurried prayer. There were prayers, yes, and tears. But there was practical help, too: card showers, a fund drive, and now, help with appearance. Most important, they are offering Jackie their continued support and friendship.

Let those at school show Jackie compassion and understanding, not pity. Help them to see the real Jackie; the missing arm and inch-long hair haven't altered her inner self.

Please, Lord, give Laurie's fingers added skill as she works with the wig. Monday morning, let it look like Jackie's own soft, shining, golden-brown hair.

"Faith that does not result in good deeds is not real faith" (James 2:20b).

Nothing Looks Right

Saturday I felt caught in the middle of a joke that begins, "There's good news and there's bad news. . . ."

The good news came at eight in the morning from the director of a high school Computer Careers Conference. There'd been a late cancellation. Lance, chosen months earlier as an alternate delegate, was invited to attend. He'd leave Monday morning.

The bad news? Lance needed a business-type suit. For some boys, finding one would be easy. Not for Lance. At six feet plus, he's basically thin; but his broad shoulders and powerful legs make finding something that doesn't need extensive alterations almost impossible.

We went to seven stores. Coats that fit his shoulders hung like granny gowns through the body. Slacks big enough to contain his legs gapped three inches through the waist.

After the fifth store I remembered (was it coincidence?) a friend who hates to shop. When she absolutely must go, she asks the Lord to help and trusts Him to guide her to the best buys on whatever she needs. Since I, too, profess to believe God is interested in every detail of our lives, no matter how small, I sat down on a bench in the mall and silently prayed.

At the seventh store we found a beautiful brown flannel suit cut western style. The coat fit perfectly except for being an inch too short in the sleeves. While the alteration personnel didn't normally work on weekends, it just happened that one of the ladies was in the store. She lengthened the sleeves and took the extra inch out of the pants before closing time.

So often, shopping for a teenager's clothing is an ordeal for parent and child. I remember when Laurie was thirteen—too small for a woman's size three, but too old (and slim) for a girl's fourteen. My cousin's son is seventeen and wants men's styling, but at 5'5", he's usually stuck with choosing clothes in the boys' department. Several girls in Laurie's class are overweight. The half sizes they need are far too matronly.

I'm so thankful, Lord, that clothing designers are becoming aware of people with special needs—the too-large, the too-small, the handicapped. It's great, too, that more and more stores are willing to carry these "different" lines.

Please, Lord, give parents—all of us—extra measures of patience and grace on those days when "nothing looks right." Give us strength to trot from store to store, and even greater strength to help us hold our tongues. Let us learn to rely on you in these small matters, as well as larger ones.

Right now I'm especially grateful that we found Lance a suit. And, Lord, bless the seamstress who was willing to work overtime to make it perfect.

"And if God provides clothing for the flowers that are here today and gone tomorrow, don't you suppose that he will provide clothing for you doubters?" (Luke 12:28).

She Walks in Beauty

Today they take pictures for the school yearbook. Instead of the usual jeans or slacks, Laurie wore a full-skirted, victorian-look dress in the same shade of blue as her eyes. She'd piled her dark hair on top of her head, allowing a few tendrils to escape and frame her face.

She was so beautiful! As I watched her leave, a lump came in my throat, tears to my eyes.

I lingered over my coffee, thinking back to the not-so-long-ago day when Laurie's beauty was only a faint promise; to those early teen years of braces, glasses, knobby knees, and an occasional "zit" on her face. It was a trying time, and she often despaired. "Braces make my lips stick out!" she'd wail. Or, "These horrible glasses make me look deformed!" Or "I'll be the only high school senior in the entire world who is 30-30-30!"

Life and Laurie went on. The braces came off, revealing straight, white teeth, not to mention the correct bite so essential for the health of those teeth. She was popular while wearing glasses as well as later, when she changed to contact lenses. In the process, she learned that friendliness and a pleasant personality are the real beauty secrets. She gained a figure that is firm, well-proportioned, and right for her height. She even has a knack for doing her hair, and has an innate fashion sense, neither of which came from me.

I know that youth and beauty and physical perfection don't last. But a feeling of beauty is essential to a teenager's self-image! We, as parents, need to be aware of this fact, rather than chalking it up to "vanity." For which of us is without our own particular vanities?

Some Christians really struggle with the issue of physical attractiveness. Certainly, we can go overboard, especially where our children are concerned. We can put so much emphasis on their having the latest hairdos and most fashionable clothes that we neglect other, more important things. Some people even make physical perfection (their own or their children's) into a god.

Surely, though, Lord, you don't object when we try to make the most of the attributes you have given us. After all, you in your divine wisdom put into us the desire to be attractive. And you knew that the desire would be at its strongest during the teen years.

Keep me—keep all parents—from being overly concerned with our children's appearances, from overemphasizing that facet of life. On the other hand, don't let us neglect those things we can afford that make such a difference to our teens—things like braces, hair styling, blemish medicine, even contact lenses.

You know that my love for Laurie (as your love for me) doesn't depend on her looks. Still, I sing a song of thanksgiving for this lovely young woman you have given to be my daughter. As she matures, I ask that she develops inner loveliness and strength of character. Without these, true beauty is impossible.

I add this prayer for all teenagers, everywhere: let them *feel* beautiful! Let them be seen through the eyes of love, for those eyes make everything lovely.

"Charm can be deceptive and beauty doesn't last, but a woman who fears and reverences God shall be greatly praised" (Prov. 31:30).

7

Laurie and Friends

Bored, Blue, Nothing to Do

Laurie has little spare time during the school year. She's usually so busy, a few hours alone at home are considered prime time. But this is the third day school has been closed because of heavy snow, and all related activities have been cancelled. Unnecessary travel is strongly discouraged, and it's much too nasty to go anywhere anyway.

Laurie slept late, cleaned her room, and helped me with lunch. This afternoon she puttered—writing letters, baking cookies, reading and listening to the radio, trying out different combinations of clothing.

"This wasn't exactly the most exciting day of my life," she commented at supper. "Sometimes I like to be alone, but after a while I get bored without my friends."

Loneliness and boredom are part of life. The most glamorous jobs have tedious periods. Sports heros and film stars find themselves without companions or admirers. According to statistics, most women will spend the later years of their lives by themselves. But in every age, every group, every occupation, the happiest people are those who have learned to be content alone.

Friends are important, of course. Sharing activities with them multiplies the fun, and our lives would be dull without their companionship. But learning to be alone is important, too.

That's why we've never allowed Laurie or Lance to fill every waking moment with group activities. They can't have (or be) company every night, and we don't drive them here or there simply because they're bored without friends. We also encourage hobbies. Laurie doesn't do beautiful crochet like Beth, and she can't cartoon like Kerri, but she writes lovely poetry, enjoys reading, and spends time perfecting and taping songs.

Times alone are vital for the refreshment of our spirits. Even Jesus sometimes went away from the crowd. Certainly it's possible to pray with others, and group Bible study is beneficial. But deep thinking and serious conversations with the Father require solitude.

Lord, as I look back on my own life I'm thankful I learned, as a teenager, to enjoy many solitary activities. Walking, riding horses, playing the piano, reading—these are things I used to fill long summer hours, but which still delight me today.

Help Laurie, and all teens, to learn that there are times when they will be alone and bored, when nothing seems fun or even interesting. Teach them that these times come to us all, and let them learn to make the most of such solitude.

Guide Laurie, Lord, and help her develop her inner resources, so that alone or with others, she'll be the well-rounded person you planned.

"As soon as Jesus heard the news, he went off by himself in a boat to a remote area to be alone" (Matt. 14:13a).

Left Out

Laurie's clock was set for eight Saturday morning. She'd allowed just enough time to dress and gulp a bowl of cereal before she would leave to decorate the gym for the school's annual Spring Fling.

About ten minutes after the alarm went off she yelled, "Come here! Quick!"

I rushed to her room. Dressed in undies only, she was standing in front of the mirror staring at some ominous-looking pink blotches that dotted her arms, legs, and midriff. I found a few more on her back, and while we searched, the first spot appeared on her face.

"Looks like hives," I told her. "Have you eaten anything unusual or tried a new cosmetic or perfume?"

"Nothing!" she wailed. Her voice rose to a hysterical pitch. "How can I go anywhere looking like this? Do you realize this is my first date with Greg in two months? He must like me again or he wouldn't have asked for tonight, and if I can't go he'll find someone else, and—"

"Maybe the doctor can do something," I interrupted. "Or maybe the hives will go away by themselves. Lots of times they do."

But Laurie's didn't. The doctor gave her a cortisone shot, extra-strength antihistamines, and ointment. The medicines helped control the awful itching, but by midafternoon Laurie's face was so swollen her eyes were narrow slits. Her normally slender fingers looked like fat, puffy sausages.

She cried, called Greg and cancelled the date, then cried again. I'd expected her to spend the hours between seven and midnight in tears. Actually, the antihistamines made her so drowsy it took the edge off her physical *and* emotional pain. It helped, too, that Beth stopped by twice. Greg didn't even call. He'd brought a date from out-of-town, Beth reported, and was doing his best to avoid all Laurie's friends.

By Sunday afternoon Laurie's swelling had subsided a bit and the blotches were beginning to fade. Beth and Laurie spent an hour (I suspended the thirteen-minute rule) on the telephone. I assumed Laurie was getting all the details from the night before, but she surprised me.

"I was telling Beth how miserable and left out I'd felt," she said, "when I realized that lots of other kids probably sat home feeling the same way. You have to have a date for the Fling, so lots of kids are totally out in the cold. Beth and I are going to petition the Student Council to change the rules. There's got to be some way we could include everyone who wants to come. Besides, it's old-fashioned to require a date!''

Lord, I never thought I'd thank you that Laurie had hives on Fling night, but I do. Thanks—joyfully, exuberantly, from the depths of my heart! Laurie knows how it hurts to be left out, and she's going to do something for others in the same situation. Is the word empathy, Lord? Feeling what others feel?

Whatever the name, I'm glad that, sometimes, Laurie has it.

"When others are happy, be happy with them. If they are sad, share their sorrow" (Rom. 12:15).

Families Together

"Mom, Jon's on the phone!" Laurie hollered early Saturday morning. "His dad is taking him and Kiki fishing, and I'm invited. May I go?"

"What you catch, you clean!" I hollered back.

"What I catch, I give to Jon!" she responded.

I was a little surprised at Laurie's enthusiasm—surprised but glad. Laurie and Jon have been special to each other for so long I'd hate to see them drift apart just because Laurie is a sophomore and Jon (two years and one week younger) is still in junior high.

Our families are close and the children have grown up more as cousins than friends. Jon's mother attended Laurie's first music contest in my place, and Laurie's gone on many of their family vacations. I was Jon's first babysitter, Laurie his first friend. When Kiki (five at the time) found out Laurie was adopted, she cried.

"Why didn't *you* get Laurie first, Mom?" she scolded her mother. "Then she could have been *my* sister instead of Lance's!"

They've had so many good times. I remember the three of them at Grandma's farm; they promised not to get in the pond, but came back covered with mud "from the edge." Just two years ago, during a terrible storm, I caught Laurie and Jon dashing outside to see who could find the biggest hailstone. Jon tells Laurie which of her boyfriends are "cool" and which are "creeps"; she helps him plan for the big class party.

A few weeks ago she confided that she had a better time with Jon than with some of the boys she dated. "I don't have to dress up or do my hair," she explained. "We like things some older guys think are dumb, like shooting baskets at the community center or just sitting in the same room reading books. I guess the main thing, though, is that when we fight I don't worry that it will break up the friendship. We've fought lots of times before, and are still friends."

I'm glad, Lord, that Laurie has friends of different ages. When teens automatically shut themselves off from contact with those older or younger, they miss out on some valuable relationships. This is especially true when boys and girls see each other only as potential date material. Please, keep Laurie from even thinking she has outgrown her younger friends, or from feeling she has nothing in common with those decades older.

Thank you for Jon and Kiki and their family, Lord, and also for Beth and hers! It is a wonderful thing when whole families are friends, when everyone likes everyone. It is a rare and special blessing that has enriched us all.

"[Jesus'] parents didn't miss him the first day, for they assumed he was with friends among the other travelers" (Luke 2:43b, 44a).

Wet Blanket

Laurie and Kerri hit the ceiling when they read the room assignments for the church ski trip.

"They've stuck Velda in with us!" Laurie wailed. "She'll ruin everything!"

"Don't be silly," I scolded. "Others are in the same kind of situation. The two women I'll be with aren't close friends, and your father is with men he hardly knows. We expect to manage fine. Besides, one person can't spoil the trip."

"Velda can," Kerri said flatly. "She never smiles, never likes anything, complains constantly, and thinks everything we do is a sin."

"Oh? Like what?"

Kerri ticked off items on her fingers: "Laughing, talking about boys, watching *General Hospital*, reading *Seventeen*. . . ."

"Not to mention bowling and wearing eye shadow," Laurie chimed in, batting her mauve-frosted lids at me.

"No one could be that awful," I said firmly. "Velda is probably shy or insecure. If you girls will be friendly and include her—"

Laurie rolled her eyes back in her head. "Mom, no one can stand being around her long enough to be friendly! Did it ever occur to you that some people just have rotten personalities?"

"And Velda is one of them," Kerri said.

That was a week ago, and we're home from the trip. After four days with Velda, I've learned two things. First, one wet blanket *can* put a damper on *everyone's* fun. Second, some people do have rotten personalities, and Velda is one of them. (Not in God's sight, I'm sure. But He can see things we can't.) Even our pastor lost patience with her.

Velda's narrow theology was part of the problem; everything we did was in some way sinful. Kerri's ski pants were indecently tight. (She'd borrowed them from Beth. They were snug, but *not* indecent.) The restaurants where we ate at night, and every eating place on the ski slopes served wine and beer. (The only place in town that didn't was Hot Dog Haven. I'm sure the Lord understood.) Pastor didn't make evening devotions mandatory. (Velda cornered him and insisted he should take attendance and send truants home in disgrace.)

If those things weren't bad enough, she was also a chronic complainer. The bus was uncomfortable. The Lodge was too far from the slopes. The instructors weren't friendly. The weather was too cold. The lift ran too fast. Laurie skiied too fast and talked to people she didn't know in the lift lines. The hamburgers didn't taste like the kind from McDonald's.

Lord, we believe the biblical portrait of you is accurate, so we believe you were a man who enjoyed life. You had many friends—righteous and sinners alike. People even called you a drunk and a glutton. You must have been pleasant and smiled often because children sat on your knee and people of all ages flocked to be near you.

Why are some Christians unable to follow your example? They seem to think being gloomy and being spiritual are one and the same! Certainly, temptations to sin are everywhere. But must we become so hung up on sin that we can't even enjoy the fellowship of other Christians?

Thank you that Laurie isn't a gloom-and-doom Christian. That type rarely attracts followers. Help Laurie and Kerri and their friends to show compassion toward Velda. Guard their tempers and preserve their sense of humor when they are around her. Let them realize that Velda is, in a way, more handicapped than Howie, who is retarded.

Be with Velda, too. Enable her to break free of the chains that keep her from experiencing your joy. Help her to enjoy the abundant life you have promised. Surely that is the way you want your children to live!

"For the kingdom of God is not a matter of eating and drinking, but of righteousness, peace and joy in the Holy Spirit" (Rom. 14:17, NIV).

Rita's Pregnant

Yesterday Laurie came home with the news that Rita is pregnant. "Mom, you can't imagine what she's going through!" she told me. "The guy's been her steady for a year, and he said he loved her! Now he acts like he doesn't know who she is!"

Rita is only three months older than Laurie. There are some big decisions she must now make. She needs to know God is still her friend, that no matter what we do He is willing to forgive and help us begin again when we come to Him in repentance.

I'm glad that Laurie is standing by her. She needs divine wisdom as she talks, and listens, to Rita. She's already given Rita the name and address of the girls' home where she was born. "I'm glad I was adopted," she explained. "I'm grateful to my birth mother for giving me life, and also for being unselfish enough to do what she felt was best for me."

As she counsels, I hope she learns from Rita's experience. Teens—Christian ones included—are human, and subject to all temptations. They can easily slip into sexual involvement and be left with consequences they never anticipated.

Laurie's words "He said he loved her" echo in my mind. Girls (and women) are just naturally more romantic than men—at least it seems that way to me. We love to be told we are loved! Phrases such as "You're so beautiful!" or "You are the only one for me" or "I love you so much I'd never hurt you" are music to our ears. The problem is, boys don't always mean these love words as seriously (or for as long) as girls take them.

I've reminded Laurie of this. Not to make boys seem like monsters, but simply to point out the very real differences in male and female points of view when it comes to love, sex, and romance. I want Laurie prepared to react to "love talk" with a little healthy skepticism. I also want her to have the self-assurance to respond, "If you *really* loved me, you wouldn't want me to do anything wrong."

Some Christians try to stop premarital sex by preventing (or trying to!) any contact between the sexes. They believe dating, holding hands, and kissing good-night are wrong. A prominent Bible college even prohibits boys and girls from talking together outside class unless a chaperone is present.

I don't agree with this approach. It doesn't work. It encourages sneaking around, and it causes young people to miss some valuable friendships. I'm glad Lance and Laurie date. They have fun, they gain social poise, and their experiences now will help them make wiser choices when it's time to consider a lifemate.

Lord, it's so difficult to grow up today, so much harder than in my time, when there was a well-defined line that "good girls" didn't cross. Growing up is hard for today's parents, too. I know I have trouble accepting the fact that Laurie (my baby!) is physically mature, with natural, God-given sex drives.

Deliver me from the temptation to keep her a little girl, from hindering her as she struggles toward adulthood. But, Lord, help her realize that while sex is a gift from you, it's to be used only within the framework of marriage.

Let her use this marvelous gift in your way, in your time.

"But sexual sin is never right: our bodies were not made for that, but for the Lord, and the Lord wants to fill our bodies with himself" (1 Cor. 6:13b).

The Snobs

Two incidents this week have caused me to take a look at my own relationship with the Lord, even though both of them concerned Laurie.

The school music department has a mixed ensemble that is often asked to entertain various clubs and groups, as well as perform at festivals and contests. Laurie and Beth were in the group last year, so are assured of being included again.

There are some openings, though, and an extremely obese and unattractive girl announced her intention to try out for a place. Laurie and Beth promptly appointed themselves a committee of two to see that she didn't succeed.

"She has a lovely voice," they casually mentioned to both music teachers and everyone else concerned. "But people *see* us before they *hear* us, so our appearance is terribly important."

When selections were made, the girl wasn't included.

A few days later Laurie and Kerri were discussing a new boy in their Sunday school class. He's interested in Kerri, but she stays as far away from him as possible.

"He's really awful!" she said. "Hair about an eighth of an inch long, jeans pulled up over his stomach . . ."

"And those horrible, black-rimmed glasses!" Laurie added, making a face.

I suggested he was probably lonely. "You don't have to date him, but surely you can sit by him at church and introduce him around."

"Not me," Kerri said.

"Or me," Laurie agreed. "I'd die before I'd be seen hanging around a creep like that."

I'm afraid Laurie is a snob. She clings to her own group. She judges people on the basis of what they wear, how they talk, whether they are cool. It disturbs me that she so often hangs a "socially unacceptable" label on anyone who doesn't meet her rigid standards. Does a guy wear high-water jeans? He's a scuzzie. Is a girl fat? Gross—and out.

It's both normal and desirable to have special friends. Chemistry or mutual interests or some entirely unknown factor draws us to some people, keeps us distant from others. Even Jesus had an inner circle—Peter, James, and John, the beloved. I know that fear and insecurity and peer pressure keep teens from crossing cultural and other boundaries. But snobbery—this looking down on those who are different, labeling them inferior—is not God's way.

Lord, even as I scold the girls, I know the problem is not Laurie's alone. For I am brought face to face with the knowledge that, in the secret places of my heart, I too am a snob.

I described a woman in our church as "having the mentality of a houseplant." I hoped a friend would be unable to attend a formal concert with me, simply because she always wore broken-down loafers and socks instead of heels and hose. I sang with a quartet before a group of prominent businesswomen, but I didn't concentrate on communicating your message because the singer standing next to me was wearing a stained, dirty dress. I was afraid her slovenliness would be a bad reflection on me.

Laurie is a snob, Lord, and so am I. Please, forgive us both. Help me set a better example of tolerance and love. Let me be careful that the attitudes and actions she sees in me reflect your goodness. May we realize that all people are made in your image and for that reason are worthy of respect.

"For God treats everyone the same" (Rom. 2:11).

Howie

I was sitting on the front porch when Howie came up the walk. Technically, he's in Laurie's class at school; in fact, he attends special sessions for the slightly retarded.

"Brain damage at birth," his mother once told me. She went on to express hope that Howie would eventually be able to live alone and hold a job. "With God's help he's already progressed much further than anyone thought possible!" Her optimism, her gratitude for the slightest gain is truly humbling.

Howie was clearly uncomfortable. His face was bright red and he shifted his weight from foot to foot as he spoke. "Is Laurie home?" he asked.

"I think so, Howie. I'll go get her."

Laurie's reaction was predictable. "Howie? What's he want?"

"I have no idea."

She followed me outdoors and took Howie to the bamboo swing several yards from my chair. Howie doesn't talk softly, and I could hear the conversation.

"Uh, Laurie, would you go to the church party with me Saturday night?"

My heart nearly stopped! What would Laurie say? Howie has been hurt so many times. People pretend he isn't there or talk about him as if he were deaf! I know Laurie isn't interested in dating him, and it would be unfair to encourage him to think otherwise. But if Laurie laughs I'll shake her until her teeth rattle.

"Howie, it's really nice of you to ask," Laurie's words floated across the yard. "I've already told Mike I'll go with him, but I'll see you there."

"Yeah. That's okay." After a minute he said, "What about some other time? Can I take you some place?"

Laurie's voice was unexpectedly gentle. "Let's just keep being friends. I'll see you Sunday nights at youth group. And you and Beth and Mike and I can still eat together at the cafeteria on Wednesdays."

The arrangement must have been okay. Howie visited another five or ten minutes. When he left, Laurie sat down beside me.

"Did you hear?"

I nodded. "You handled it very well."

"Don't tell anyone," she requested. "If people knew, they'd tease Howie until he was miserable."

"I promise. What's this about lunch on Wednesdays?"

"That's the only day I have lunch period the same time as Howie," Laurie explained. "It started about three months ago. A bunch of us were eating when Howie came up and spoke to me. He was going to sit down when Greg said, 'Hey, no retards allowed at this table. Go sit with the other dummies!' "

Her voice shook with indignation. "Mom, Howie had tears in his eyes, and Greg just laughed! Beth looked at me, and I looked at her, and we both picked up our trays and sat with Howie. Now Mike usually eats with us, and sometimes Kerri or someone else."

With that, she went back to whatever she'd been doing before Howie came.

Lord, I've underestimated Laurie. I was so hung up on what I considered snobbery I didn't even look for times when she was compassionate and understanding. Thank you that decency took precedence over Greg—that Laurie's eyes were opened to the kind of person Greg is. (Is that why he's out of the picture, Lord? Whatever the reason, I'm grateful.)

Thank you that Laurie is willing to be Howie's friend. Thank you that she and Beth and a few others had the courage to sit with him.

And when Laurie acts like a snob, Lord, let me remember today.

"Anyone who takes care of a little child like this is caring for me! And whoever cares for me is caring for God who sent me. Your care for others is the measure of your greatness" (Luke 9:48).

8

Lance and Company

A Harmless Prank

It was one of those rare Saturday nights with everyone home. Laurie was writing a term peper. Lance had delivered ice until 7:00—too late to go out with his friends.

About 10:30 the telephone rang. Lance answered, and when he hung up his hand was shaking. "Mark's at the police station," he told us. "His folks are gone, so I said we'd come down and get him."

We went, and Mark was released to come home with us. Everytime I think about what happened, I get cold chills.

There were four boys in the car. They were driving around the neighborhood when they noticed an unusually large number of yard signs in the Sheraton addition. Someone (no one is sure who) suggested they mix them up as a joke. They were replacing a "No Trespassing" with a "Four-Party Garage Sale Today" when the house lights went on and a man ran out waving a shotgun.

He grabbed Mark's arm and held the gun to his head. "Lie face down on the ground or I'll blow your brains out!" he ordered the boys. "The police can deal with you rotten punks!" He yelled to his wife to send for a squad car, and continued holding the gun on Mark until it arrived.

In the end, the man was persuaded not to press charges. The policeman knew one of the boys, and was able to convince the man this wasn't the same gang who had been bothering him. But the incident shook us all. Mark was terrified. "I was afraid to breathe for fear he'd kill me," he told us on the way home.

Lance was scared, too. "I would have been with them," he kept saying.

I was afraid for all of them—for the man who had been harassed once too often; for the boys whose silly prank (although certainly wrong) might have cost a life.

Help us to learn from this, Lord. Let me be more understanding when I hear or read of kids in trouble. Teach the boys to *think* before they act. Let your wisdom guide their recreation.

And, Lord, forgive me for being selfish, but thank you so much that Lance wasn't with them that night!

"Keep your eyes open for spiritual danger; stand true to the Lord; act like men; be strong; and whatever you do, do it with kindness and love" (1 Cor. 16:13, 14).

Caution: Cults

According to Lance, two recruiters from Children of God have been hanging around our town all week. They aren't allowed on the school grounds, but have been busy making friends at the Hub, a popular hangout.

"Several kids seem to be buying their line," Lance said. "I've read enough to know Children of God is a dangerous group, but some of the things they say sound really good." He thought a minute. "How do you tell a cult, anyway?"

"Well, they use the Bible but they redefine its terms," I said.

"They know the Scriptures backward and forward," Lance said. "Anytime Christians question them, they answer straight from the Bible."

The point is, neither of us knows as much about cults as we should. What distinguishes a cult? How do we keep people from being taken in by false claims? We called our pastor, who gave us a booklet to read plus extra copies for Lance to hand out.

I'd always thought cults preyed on those with no beliefs at all. I was wrong. They are most successful recruiting idealistic young people, some of whom are Christians, who are frustrated by the system. Such people are gullible and willing to believe anyone who promises the opportunity to help others and make the world a better place to live.

Most cults pay lip service to the Bible but actually teach things that are opposed to God's principles. For instance, Children of God may require members to break entirely with their parents and families, and even to steal money and valuables. They also promote sexual promiscuity.

Many cults are built around a strong, authoritative leader who claims he has received special, secret revelations from God. Members of the Unification Church (Moonies) are virtually enslaved by their devotion to Sun Myung Moon. Every moment of their time is programmed. They cease to think for themselves, often becoming more like robots than people. Many literally work themselves to exhaustion to follow Moon's exhortation to work for the kingdom. (He, like many cult leaders, lives in unbelievable luxury, while his followers barely survive.)

Cults teach salvation by works, and/or salvation through contributions to the cult. Financial exploitation of members is common. Most cultists aren't actually sure *what* they believe, but many deny the deity of Christ.

Unfortunately, recognizing the marks of a cult isn't enough to prevent teens from being deceived by its claims. According to our pastor, the most important thing we can do as parents is to make sure our children receive sound biblical teaching. They must know and understand the doctrinal basis for our faith. They must know what God's Word teaches; what the church as Christ's body represents; and what Christ requires of those who follow Him.

Thank you, Lord, that our church provides the teaching we need to grow spiritually. Thank you for a pastor who cares about young people. (He has met with other ministers and arranged for a mature Christian to be at the Hub as long as these cultists remain in town.)

Thank you, too, for Lance's concern. Give him your wisdom as he hands out the booklets and tries to refute false claims. Strengthen those who are tempted, and free those in bondage. Let them use their idealism, their youthful high spirits, to work for a better world, but always, only, under your guiding hand.

"But there were false prophets, too, in those days, just as there will be false teachers among you" (2 Pet. 2:1a).

Jason's Folks Have Split Up

"Mom, could Jason stay here for a few days?" Lance asked.

It should have been a routine question, but something told me it wasn't.

"Of course. Are his folks gone?"

"They've split up. Permanently." Lance's voice cracked, and tears fogged the lenses of his glasses.

I was stunned. It simply couldn't be! Jason's parents had been married twenty-five years! They were Christians!

"Are you sure?" I asked.

Lance took a deep breath and told me what he knew. "Jason's dad left for a business trip two weeks ago. Or that's what he told Jason. Last night he came and picked up all his clothes. It seems he's had an apartment—and a girlfriend—in the Brittany Complex for over a year."

"Jason's mother is probably in shock," I said. "Shouldn't he stay with her?"

"She's going to visit her sister until things blow over. Jason shouldn't miss that much school, and he doesn't want to be alone right now."

"He's welcome to stay with us as long as he likes."

After Lance left I put sheets on the extra bunk in his room and did several other chores, moving through the house in a zombie-like trance. What caused this seemingly stable marriage to disintegrate? Didn't Jason's parents consider his feelings? Or God's?

Wondering is pointless, though. Right now I need to help Jason cope with the situation. Only I'm not sure how.

I guess I start by making him feel welcome, and by being available if he wants to talk. (He probably will. He and Lance and I have talked several times.) Oh, for the right words! I must remind him he isn't to blame for this break-up. I know it sounds odd, but most teens harbor guilt that they are (indirectly, at least) the cause of their parents' problems.

I musn't utter a word of blame or censure. God hates divorce, but He continues to love those involved. And only He knows the pressures and pains that led to this drastic step.

Father, be with Jason right now, at this moment when he is so alone. Help him to see that his parents aren't abandoning him, even though it may seem that way. Assure him you won't abandon him, either—not him, not them.

Let me use this situation to assure Lance and Laurie that their family won't be broken by divorce. You know, Lord, that our marriage isn't perfect, or even perfectly happy. Lance and Laurie are aware of the quarrels their father and I have had, the disagreements that are sometimes bitter. Let me show them the other side, too, the underlying love that sustains us through dark times. Help me to be more openly loving, more affectionate, more reassuring.

Help me, also, to teach them that the key to a lasting marriage isn't beauty or money or sexual attraction or even love. It is commitment—commitment to each other, to the sanctity of marriage, and to you.

"For from the very first he made man and woman to be joined together permanently in marriage" (Mark 10:6b).

Psycho

"Jason's mother is in the psychiatric ward at St. Anthony's," Lance told me yesterday. "Jason wasn't in school, and rumors are flying all over that she's gone completely crazy."

Later that evening I went to a church meeting. Whatever rumors were at school were surely kind compared to the comments I heard whispered among Christians: "If she had trusted God, this wouldn't have happened." "I don't understand people who can't get hold of themselves." "I always thought she was a Christian, but evidently she isn't."

I was incensed! Would we say of a person with pneumonia or gallstones, "If she were a Christian she wouldn't have become ill"? At the same time, I didn't know what to say except meaningless platitudes—"We all need help sometimes."

Thankfully, Pastor was willing to confront issues head-on. It seems that Jason's mother is suffering from depression, not surprising in the light of what she has gone through. She *chose* to be hospitalized; with intensive treatment she could be home in ten days and probably fully recovered in a few weeks.

Pastor explained that mental and emotional problems come to Christians and non-Christians alike. They are not a measure of spirituality (or lack of it). They are not a sign of failure. Extreme stress can cause the most Christlike among us to buckle. He emphasized that if more people sought help for minor problems, there would be fewer major ones. He reminded us that Luke was a physician, and that Christ himself said those who were *sick* needed a physician.

Dear Lord, this divorce has been extremely traumatic for Jason's mother. I can only imagine that she reacted as I might have. During an actual crisis I am a rock. Afterward, I crumble like gravel.

Please touch her with your healing hand. Thank you for the courage she had to ask for help. There have been times when I, too, have needed it, but was too proud to ask.

Give Jason a double measure of your love. It's good the family was open about the matter. It's impossible for a child or teenager to deal with the unknown. The known, no matter how bad, can be handled. Jason has talked with his mother and with her doctor. He knows this illness isn't his fault, that it's the result of stress from the marriage breakup. All the same, he needs your reassurance.

Thank you for Lance's concern. This morning we discussed ways he could help. Jason's coming back here to stay, and we'll be available to listen when he needs to talk. Lance will also try to correct misinformation. He can counter "Jason's mother went crazy!" with a calm, "No, she didn't. She's suffering from depression, and will be fine soon. Lots of people have the same thing, but refuse to get help."

Dear God, you know I've also had bouts with depression. I never thought I'd thank you for them, but now I do. Because I understand.

"How long must I be hiding daily anguish in my heart?" (Ps. 13:2a).

Ken's Getting Married

Lance had been invited to Preview Weekend at North College, and was really excited about the trip. On Tuesday, though, he asked me to cancel his reservation.

"Why?" I asked. "You've been looking forward to it."

"I know. But Ken's getting married Saturday night, and he's asked me to be his best man."

"Ken? Getting married? He's younger than you!" Sunday afternoon Ken had played two-on-two with Lance, Jason, and Mark. A couple of weeks earlier he'd been teasing Laurie and Beth about their costumes for Fifties Day at school—with his sleeves rolled up and his hair greased back, he looked younger than they did. "I didn't know Ken had a serious girlfriend."

"He's got a girl—and a kid on the way." Lance hesitated, wondering how much to tell me. "Her folks want her to have an abortion. Ken's folks figure it's her problem, and are dead set against him marrying her. They were furious when he admitted the baby was his. At any rate, neither set of parents plans to attend the wedding, so Ken is pretty much alone."

I suppose I should have taken the opportunity to talk with Lance, to reiterate our views—and God's—that premarital sex leads to heartbreak. It's wrong, not because God wants to deprive teens of fun, but because of the enormous amount of damage it does, and because it contradicts His principles of marriage.

I didn't say any of those things to Lance. My concern was for Ken, his bride, their unborn child. Their lives will never be the same. Ken won't be teasing Laurie or playing basketball with Lance anymore. The girl will have to forget about slumber parties and the Fling. I pray that his (or her) parents will help support them until they finish high school.

They are so young, Lord! Yet Ken is showing maturity that many boys don't have. He is willing to accept responsibility for the life that is to be, even though his parents urge him to think solely of himself. Thank you that he and his bride-to-be had the courage to refuse abortion. I can't believe two wrongs make a right, although I'll admit that abortion would certainly make things easier.

Marriage isn't always wise. But Lance says they love each other, and really want to be married. I pray for the marriage, Father, and for their lives together. Strengthen their love with your own.

They will need support. Half of all teenage marriages end in divorce within five years. And when such marriages do last, the cost is often great: loss of youth, freedom, fun, even college and career plans.

Our family is invited to the wedding, Lord, and we're

going. After the ceremony we're hosting a small dinner party for Ken. We hope to show this young couple the support their parents refuse, the support they so desperately need.

Bless them, Lord. With your help, they can prove the statistics on teen marriage wrong.

"Share each other's troubles and problems, and so obey our Lord's command" (Gal. 6:2).

Joe Nobody

Last night, Lord, a classmate of Lance's killed himself. He drove home from school, ate supper with his family, then went to his room and shot himself through the head. He left a note on the desk: "You all seem to think I'm special. I know better. I'm empty inside, and one day everybody will find that out."

He signed it, "Joe Nobody."

"Did you know him?" I asked Lance. "The name is familiar, but I can't place him."

"He was an All-League guard and had been offered a football scholarship to State," Lance said. "In fact, he seemed to have everything going for him. He was a good athlete, always on the Honor Roll, a candidate for Outstanding Senior—everything."

He buried his face in his hands. A few minutes later he said, "Mom, all day I kept wondering if I could have helped him. I always assumed he had plenty of friends, so I never tried to get close. I don't even know if he was a Christian. I keep thinking if I'd tried to be a friend, Joe might be alive right now."

"Joe's death isn't your fault, Lance," I said. "It isn't humanly possible to be friends with everyone." My words weren't adequate, but I didn't know what else to say.

I don't want Lance to suffer from an exaggerated sense of guilt or despair. At the same time, I want him to be sobered by this tragedy. Suicide is the second leading cause of death among teens; only auto accidents take more lives. There are thousands like Joe who are literally dying inside. Suicide isn't confined to those who don't know Christ, either; Christians do it, too.

We'll probably never know why Joe took his own life. Experts list many possible causes of suicide: loneliness, excessive pressure to succeed and consequent feelings of failure, poor physical health, drug abuse, and stress. But they can't explain why one person takes these things in stride, while another is driven to acute despair.

Suicide is on the rise throughout the world. Knowing that, we all need to be aware of telltale signs. The old myth "Those who talk about it don't do it" is just that—a myth. Eight out of ten people who actually kill themselves have given definite warning of their intentions. Giving away treasured possessions and preoccupations with death are other indications that a teen may be planning to end his life. Signals also come through a change in personality: a studious, high-principled boy begins cutting classes; a fashion-conscious girl refuses to bathe or wash her hair.

We can learn to recognize the signs. We can get help for teens who are troubled. But we can't always prevent it. At least at the time of the actual act, suicides are truly "not themselves." They are disturbed mentally and emotionally in a way that only God can understand.

Comfort Joe's parents and family, Lord. Their grief is intensified by the guilt they feel—like Lance's, a thousand times multiplied. "Where did we go wrong? Was there some clue we missed? Could we have prevented this?" They'll be asking these questions the rest of their lives.

Please, Lord, reach out to those who are contemplating suicide at this moment. Touch them with your love and concern. Let them see life as good and exciting and worth living.

Let Lance reach out, too. Let him offer encouragement to the classmate who is worried; invite the newcomer to "come along for a Coke"; smile at a stranger who seems down.

They are little things, I know. But sometimes little things make a big difference.

"The Lord is close to those whose hearts are breaking; he rescues those who are humbly sorry for their sins" (Ps. 34:18).

Our Hero

Laurie was setting the table when Lance came in from track practice. The minute she saw him she clapped her head to her forehead and pretended to faint.

"He's home! Our hero! Quick, someone! Blow a trumpet or something!"

"Cut it out, Laurie," Lance said disgustedly. "You're being ridiculous."

"What's going on?" I asked.

"Haven't you heard?" Laurie's voice oozed with teasing. "Lance is a hero. All the seventh-grade boys want to be just like him."

I wouldn't have blamed Lance if he'd strangled her with an athletic sock, but he was evidently too tired. He drained a glass of iced tea, grabbed a handful of carrot sticks to tide him over until supper, then sprawled on the living room floor with the newspaper.

According to Laurie, the "hero" business began when some junior high students wanted to work out with the team. Lance and Jason took time to show them how to use starting blocks, stop watches, and were willing to palaver while they jogged.

That explained a lot of things: the cheering section both boys had at last week's track meet, the calls from someone who needed "to talk to Lance about practice," the extra packs of gum he's been buying.

Later I asked Lance, "Do you ever get tired of having a fan club?"

He laughed. "Sometimes. When I've spent ten minutes looking for a kid's lost duffle bag, who then remembers he forgot to bring it. Or when Jase and I end up driving all over town to take kids home because it's starting to rain. But then I think of the guys who did the same things for me."

He looked at me. "Remember Ron Freeman? He won state in the mile. He's one of the reasons I never started smoking. He even visited me in the hospital the time I broke my arm on hurdles."

Lord, I'm glad Lance is willing to befriend those who are younger. The ability to encourage others is one trait all of us should try to develop. It was Barnabas, "son of encouragement," who brought Paul to the apostles after his conversion, and who assisted him in his early ministry. It was Barnabas who wasn't willing to give up on young John Mark.

But being an encourager (I don't like the word "hero") carries a price. It means Lance has a responsibility to make his words and actions worthy of being copied, not just at track practice, but all the time. It means *continuing* to help the boys, instead of losing interest when the novelty wears off. It means demonstrating good sportsmanship, whether he wins or loses.

I guess, Lord, it boils down to letting your light shine through his life.

Please help Lance (and all of us) to be a good influence on those around us. Thank you, too, for Ron and the other "older guys" who provided a pattern for Lance. He's passing it on, Lord, and I'm confident some of those younger boys will do the same.

"And you should follow my example, just as I follow Christ's" (1 Cor. 11:1).

9

Those Who Touch Young Lives

Bless the Teachers

Laurie's trouble with her history teacher has finally been resolved. Mrs. Kincaid asked that Laurie be transferred to another section. I don't know what reason she gave, but Laurie is delighted. She's already received two "A's," and it looks as if she'll be able to stay on the Honor Roll.

I've been so concerned with this problem that I've neglected to be thankful for the other wonderful teachers Lance and Laurie have had through the years. There have been some poor ones, of course, but many have been dedicated, caring, and competent. They've had a profound and positive effect on my children's lives.

There was the math teacher who worked with Laurie after school when she was having trouble "getting" algebra, and the coach who was Lance's friend as well as instructor. There was the sixth-grade music teacher who convinced Laurie she could sing, and that young man right out of college who sparked Lance's interest in computers.

I'm grateful for the teachers they liked, Heavenly Father, and also for some they didn't. Lance hated junior English, but he gained an understanding of literature that will add an extra dimension to his life. Laurie thinks her biology instructor is too strict, too demanding, and too old-fashioned. Yet she is *learning* under him, and the discipline has been good for her.

School, with its diversity of teachers and teaching styles, is good preparation for life. I thank you that my children have this opportunity. Help them, help us all, appreciate our educational system.

Please, bless those fine men and women who teach—especially those who bring Jesus into the class with them.

"Lead me; teach me; for you are the God who gives me salvation" (Ps. 25:5a).

Faraway People

Laurie once went to a movie I had forbidden her to see. In it, a teenage boy became enraged when his girlfriend's parents tried to prevent him from seeing her. To prove that his love for the girl was strong and real, he attempted to burn the parents' house down.

I disciplined Laurie, and I hoped that by discussing the film she would realize how ridiculous the plot was. Instead, she and Beth and Kerri stoutly maintained it was "beautiful, truly romantic, and proved that teenage love was real, even if some adults don't think so."

In times past, those who most strongly influenced our children's lives were those nearby: friends, relatives, members of church and community. We read, we saw movies and television (depending on how far back we consider "times past"), and of course, we dreamed of lives more glamorous than our own. But we also saw reality every single day. The unmarried girl who got pregnant was bundled off in disgrace to a home or distant relative; her life and reputation suffered serious setbacks. The person who divorced was lonely and pathetic; he didn't find an exciting new mate within a month of his separation. The man who abused alcohol was considered a drunk; he was an object of pity, not funny or even a man of the world.

Through today's mass media, our children are influenced by people we don't know, people whose standards are often opposed to God's clear-cut guidelines. They paint pictures of life that are totally unrealistic, but some teens buy them hook, line and sinker.

Lord, there are times (like after the movie incident) when I feel I'm fighting an uphill battle to protect my children from the false promises of the world. Guide me, please, as I try to do the things I can which will keep us near you.

Keep me from arguing or shouting or making derogatory remarks. Help me, instead, to be sure Lance and Laurie receive sound teaching in our home and church. Let me quietly point out that the glamorous lives and places portrayed on television are imaginary; they simply do not exist. Let me guide them to the better films (and there are some marvelous ones) and books that are exciting *and* realistic.

Lord, when I read reviews of some of the filth that is turned loose on our young people, I am enraged. I honestly feel I could strangle those who would deliberately seek to pervert and harm innocent millions. Yet I know that isn't your way; that I must pray for them instead. So please, fill what must be tremendous vacuums in their lives with your goodness. Fill them so full there will be no room for garbage.

Thank you for those writers, directors, and stars who have steadfastly upheld decency and morality in their work. I know some have suffered for it. Be with them as they continue to stand and work for good.

Finally, Lord, let our network of family, church, and community be so strong that its influence will prevail. Lead us as we live for you in this world.

"Don't copy the behavior and customs of this world, but be a new and different person with a fresh newness in all you do and think. Then you will learn from your own experience how his ways will really satisfy you" (Rom. 12:2).

I Can't Believe It!

"Did you read this?" Lance asked, handing me the newspaper.

It took me a minute to find the article he meant. When I read it, I was shocked. Mr. T., a member of our church and a former youth group leader, had been arrested and charged with sexually abusing several young boys.

"I can't believe it!" I said. "They must have him confused with someone else."

"I believe it," Lance told me. "Remember when no one wanted to go to youth group? It was because he acted weird even then."

"What did he do?"

"He didn't *do* anything. But he kept trying to get guys to go places with him. Several times when Mark's folks were gone, Mr. T. offered to take him home, saying it would be a good chance for them to be together. And he followed guys into the bathroom, stuff like that."

"Lance, why didn't you tell someone?" I asked, horrified. "If we'd known . . . If Pastor had any idea . . ."

"We probably should have," Lance admitted. "Instead, we were really careful to stick together when he was around. And he was replaced before the problem got really bad. Besides, we didn't figure anyone would believe us. You know how it is when kids accuse an adult of anything."

At this moment I realize I've done absolutely nothing to prepare Lance for people like Mr. T. Laurie and I have talked about rape, and the school had a series of programs on preventing it. The girls learned to recognize and stay out of potentially dangerous situations—to keep car doors locked while driving, to check front- and backseats before getting into an empty car, to use the "buddy" system and stay in well-lighted areas. But I, and probably other parents as well, assumed my son was safe because things like this don't happen in *our* town.

Only they do. Experts tell us there is nearly as much

sexual abuse of boys as of girls, and teens are often the victims. In some major cities police report more demand for teenage male prostitutes than for girls. And it isn't a new problem; a third-grade classmate of mine was sexually abused, then murdered. His killer was never found.

I guess the first step in prevention is to make sure our young children know that no one (except the family doctor) should handle their bodies. The "dangerous stranger" myth is indeed a myth. In about seven out of ten cases, the molester is a person the child knows and trusts.

Lance's words point up something else we can do: take children's complaints seriously and investigate them. Studies show that children rarely lie about sexual molestation.

We parents should have read between the lines when Mr. T. was working with the youth. Any time kids suddenly turn against an activity (or person) they formerly enjoyed, it's up to us to try to discover the reasons why.

I confess, Lord, that my mind is filled with loathing for Mr. T. To me, sexual abuse is impossible to understand. Yet I know that with you there are no degrees of sin; we have all sinned and come far short of your standards. I know Mr. T. needs your help, and that you love him even though you hate his acts.

Let him find the counseling he needs. Let him emerge from this, clean and whole and ready to live for you. Be with his family, too—his lovely wife and children. I don't know whether this comes as a total shock, or whether they've lived in fear that he would be discovered. Regardless, I can only imagine the humiliation and shame they must be feeling.

Lord, I know we live in a world where perversions abound. Forgive me for failing to prepare Lance for this. Thank you that he and his friends sensed something wrong and stuck together. Thank you, especially, for protection during a crisis I knew nothing about.

"Be careful—watch out for attacks from Satan, your

great enemy. He prowls around like a hungry, roaring lion, looking for some victim to tear apart" (1 Pet. 5:8).

Beauty from Ashes

After eight years of waiting, a couple in our church has adopted a precious baby girl. When Pastor announced the good news, I was reminded of those special people who make so many family circles complete: adoption workers. Is there any other profession that deals with such heartbreak, yet brings so many people joy? Bless them richly, Father, for their care and dedication.

Be with the young girl who made the agonizing decision to part with her baby. She is no doubt lonely and devastated, and probably wondering if she did the right thing. Speak to her heart. Assure her this child will receive the finest care, and abundant love. Let her feel your continued presence as she picks up the pieces of her life and prepares to build again.

Bless these new parents, too, although I'm sure they feel richly blessed already. I'm tempted to write or call. There are so many things I'd like to tell them! I hope they'll always be open and honest about the adoption process, and give their daughter all the information they have. Laurie knows her mother had blue eyes, brown hair, and was beautiful. She knows her father was short, dark, and athletic. She knows everything we know, Father, and each fact helps her to know and understand herself.

I hope this family will develop a birth story and repeat it often as their child grows. Laurie still likes hearing how we carried her home in a green basket, how Lance begged to name her Cinderella, and how she already had so much hair that our first purchases were a brush and some ribbon.

Let them know that adoption makes no difference in the quantity or quality of love the child gives. Help them, also, to accept this little girl as she is. Laurie was hyperactive and cranky, but also extremely perceptive and verbal. An-

other baby may be more placid (easier on Mom!) but not
nearly so interesting. These differences occur in all children, not just adopted ones.

Don't let them be hurt by their child's curiosity about
her birth parents. Most adopted children have (at times) an
"empty" feeling. And it's no wonder! Part of their identity
is missing! But most still love their adoptive parents very
much, consider them the real parents, and feel they are better off for being adopted.

Laurie and I have learned through trial and error, Lord.
I don't suppose I would spare this family—or any—the
struggle. I'm not sure it would be wise. Conflict is part of
the growth process; resolved, it strengthens and increases
love.

But do let them take advantage of available help, especially when this child reaches the vulnerable teens. Help
them to put her in contact with other adopted children.
She'll feel less alone, and will know others who understand
how she feels. Books can help, too. Last year we bought
How It Feels to Be Adopted by Jill Krementz.* It's both
rich and realistic, and should be required reading for teens
and parents alike.

There are at least six people involved directly in an
adoption: the birth parents, the child, the adoptive parents,
and the social worker. Thank you so much for all of them.
Thank you for Laurie. I'm eternally grateful you chose her
to be ours.

Lord, when I call on these proud, new parents, let it be
with congratulations only. The time for talking will come
later.

*"To all who mourn in Israel he will give: Beauty for
ashes; joy instead of mourning; praise instead of heaviness.
For God has planted them like strong and graceful oaks for
his own glory"* (Isa. 61:3).

---

* Alfred A. Knopf, Publisher, New York, N.Y., 1982.

Those Who Make Them Feel Good

From time to time, special people have touched my children's lives. Some were friends and relatives; others, strangers. All had something in common: they helped Lance and Laurie feel good about themselves.

I've come before the Lord so many times lately with complaints, with people problems. Today I just want to thank Him for those wonderful ones who have provided understanding, or inspiration, or joy.

There was the nursery school teacher who patiently worked with hyperactive Laurie when no one else would. She mixed quiet firmness with generous portions of praise and love. She insisted Laurie obey, but didn't demand the impossible. (She didn't make Laurie shut her eyes at rest time, or sit totally still during stories, or the dozens of other things most four-year-olds could handle, but which have come to Laurie slowly—with prayer and effort.)

I'm thankful for the coach who saw a potential runner in gangly, sixth-grade Lance. After a baseball game when Lance played one inning (after the team was behind ten runs), he put his arm on Lance's shoulder. "You're not going to make a ballplayer, son," he said gently, "but I've been noticing how well you run. Have you thought about going out for the track team in junior high? I'd like to call the coach and tell him about you."

The disappointments of that whole season, and the one before, vanished in an instant.

A sportswriter provided another magic moment. After Lance lost his chance for the state track meet and a scholarship at State, the man walked over to him. "I hope you won't be discouraged," he said. "You have potential, and I think you'd enjoy running for a small school. Think about it, and let me know what you decide."

Once Laurie developed a slight infection in her left eye. It wasn't serious, but the eye was red and watery the day she was to be part of an Honors Choir made up of singers from several schools and towns. She left the house feeling ugly and despondent, but came home bubbling. Why?

"This boy sat down beside me at lunch," she said. "He picked my voice out and liked it so much he wanted to meet me!"

They spent a wonderful day talking music and getting acquainted. Although they've never dated, they write occasionally. Laurie will always remember how his "I love your voice" transformed a gloomy day.

Kiki can bring Laurie out of a blue mood by calling, then giggling over the telephone. Lance gets a lift from the boys who cheer for him at track meets. There are many other things that the "giver" may never think about: letters from a cousin, saying, "I'm proud of you!"; friendly smiles; even looks that say, "I'm glad you came."

I don't know all the people who have provided day (and life!) brighteners, Lord, but you do. Thank you for every single one of them! Please, bless them in a special way.

Help Lance and Laurie and me to pass on the kindnesses. Let our words and actions brighten the lives of those we meet. And thank you, again, for people who make others feel good about themselves.

"Timely advice is as lovely as golden apples in a silver basket" (Prov. 25:11).

The Community of Faith

Lord, I want to thank you for your Church, for those of all denominations who make up your body. I especially thank you for the people in my own church. Their influence on Lance and Laurie has made a permanent impact.

There's our pastor, Lord. You know (and I know and he knows) he isn't perfect. He doesn't have all the answers, and his family has many of the same problems mine does. Maybe it's because he doesn't think himself perfect that he is so dear to all of us. He is your man, called by you to shepherd this flock. But he's also, in Lance's words, "a real person, not just a preacher." For his practical help with our problems, I'm grateful.

Thank you, too, for the Sunday school teacher. She's come under criticism from time to time. "They" say she doesn't spend enough time preparing lessons, that she lets the teens spend too much time visiting. But she alone is willing to teach this class, and she is faithfully there week after week. She prays for her students, she entertains them in her home, and she cares. Bless her efforts, Lord, and her.

Bless our head usher, too. He never misses a Sunday. Before he retired he was custodian at the grade school. I'll never forget Lance's first day in kindergarten. I was sure he'd feel lonely and lost. After all, he didn't know anyone. But he came home beaming. "Guess who opened the doors when we got off the bus?" he asked. "The same man who takes up the collection at church! He smiled at me and said hi!"

There are many others, Lord. I'm grateful to our pastor's wife for sharing him so freely with us, and for her work directing plays and musicals. Thank you for the dear ladies who take time to compliment Laurie each time she sings. Thanks for the men; by being there they have helped Lance through times when church was called sissy by some.

This community of faith is at once comforting and challenging. It's so wonderful to be a part of it! I'm glad you led us here.

Oh, one more thing. Please, bless the organist. Frankly, she isn't very good. She plays wrong notes and at least twice a year starts the "Gloria Patria" when it's time for the "Doxology." She also plays six verses for five-stanza hymns. Help her to laugh at herself and keep playing, Lord—and perhaps find more time to practice.

You know her well. It's me!

"You are Peter, a stone; and upon this rock I will build my church; and all the powers of hell shall not prevail against it" (Matt. 16:18).

10

Lord, It's Me

Sometimes I Resent Them

Today I'm struggling with a very real problem—I resent my family. Right now I'm sick and tired of the demands they place on my time, my energy, and my emotions. I feel like a fly caught in a spider's web: the outer shell is intact, but the vital, life-giving juices have been sucked out.

It isn't the work that bothers me—the cooking, housecleaning, or chauffeuring. Lance and Laurie are accustomed to getting their own meals when I'm extra busy. They help with cleaning and learned long ago to launder their sports uniforms. I haven't had to mow the lawn since Lance was ten.

It's more a matter of attitude, their assumption that a "Mother on call" is an inalienable right. I'm angry about the mixed messages I receive. There are shouts of encouragement: "Be successful, Mom! Write that prize-winning article! Take the lead part in the Community Theater play!" But there are also whispers: "Be sure you still have time to drive Laurie to camp." "Remember, you must work in the concession stand during Lance's ball games." "You'll need to type Mark's term paper. He can't find anyone else to do it, and he'll flunk English if he turns it in handwritten. His mother *works* and can't get to it."

Lord, someone once said that the secret of a life pleasing

132

to you is this: "God first, others second, myself last." I'm sure that's true. At the same time I am so tired of being last, and being assailed by guilt for being selfish. (And I *am* selfish, Lord. I'm not the loving, caring, giving person I ought to be.)

Help me to get my priorities straight, my life in balance! Help me to live in the present and enjoy today. My children are nearly grown. All too soon they'll be gone, and no doubt I'll miss the noise and hubbub, the friends, the piles of laundry, and the dirty pizza pans.

In the meantime, Lord, could I ask a favor? I'd like a few hours to be totally alone. I need to rediscover myself.

"But many who are first now will be last then; and some who are last now will be first then" (Matt. 19:30).

Do I Love Them Too Much?

The All-School Honors Banquet was held last night. Lance received several awards, including Top at Track, Most Inspirational Athlete, and National Honor Society. Each time his name was called, I felt so full of pride and love that I wasn't sure I could keep it inside me! I wanted to stand on my chair and shout, "Look, everyone! That's my son! Isn't he great?" I didn't, of course. I sat with a fixed smile on my face throughout the program, applauding Lance no more and no less than any of the others.

I love my children all the time, in that way parents are supposed to love. But sometimes something happens to turn that rather ordinary love into a torrent of overwhelming, overflowing feeling. It's so real I can touch it, hold it, savor it.

A few of the incidents that trigger this flood of emotion are memorable, such as Lance's baptism and Laurie's wild sorrow when her cat Josie was killed. Most are commonplace, such as Lance wrestling with the dog; Laurie giving me an unexpected hug; her dark hair spread out over the pillow while she sleeps.

There are times, Lord, when I wonder if I love my children too much. You have commanded us to give *you* first place in our hearts. I'm not sure I always do. When someone has been critical of Lance or has hurt Laurie, I have the most unloving thoughts! Why, I've wanted to scream at or even hit those who cause my children pain! I haven't acted on those thoughts, but the desire was there. Is this something peculiar to me? Or do other mothers feel this way?

Help me to keep my unloving feelings in check, Lord. Remind me that we are all your children, equally precious in your sight—even those I find unlovable.

Thank you for the pleasure my children have brought, for the extra dimension and fullness they've added to my life. Help me experience my love for them, and yes, even my pride, without the slightest trace of guilt. At the same time, keep me always conscious that my love for them must never transcend my love for you.

"Jesus replied, 'Love the Lord your God with all your heart, soul, and mind' " (Matt. 22:37).

People Are Staring!

We were shopping for a pair of shoes to go with Laurie's new red and white dress. She'd drifted over to look at a display of tennis-shoe laces when I spotted some suitable shoes on a sale rack.

"Laurie! Come look at these!" I said, raising my voice slightly.

She was beside me an instant later, an anguished look on her face. "Mother!" she hissed. "Do you always have to shout? People are staring!"

She glanced at the shoes, pronounced them ugly, then hurried me out of the store. An hour and three stores later, she bought a pair practically identical to the ones I'd shown her.

There are times when Laurie is so sensitive it's ridiculous. I know it's normal for teenagers to try and disassociate themselves from their parents, that it is a necessary part of the transition from dependent childhood to independent adulthood. At the same time, it can be so irritating!

At least Laurie isn't embarrassed as often or over as many things as she was at twelve. That year nothing I did was right. I wore embarrassing clothes, had embarrassing hair, and said embarrassing things. Half of her sentences began with "Mom, I nearly died when you . . ."

My friends' experiences with their children had helped prepare me. When my sister's water pipes froze one winter, she had to wash at a coin-operated laundry. Her young teen became irrational at the thought and begged her to go when no one else would be awake—five in the morning, or midnight. "If any of my friends see you, they'll think we're too poor to have a washer and drier," the child wailed. "I'll be embarrassed to death!"

Another time, I went shopping with Beth's mother and older sister, who was then about twelve. The girl huddled miserably in the corner of the car, ducking her head each time we met another vehicle. "I'll die if anyone sees me in the backseat," she explained, "and riding with *two* mothers."

I even remember the time when I was thirteen, and accompanied my parents to the movies on a Saturday night. In the lobby I saw a boy I liked. Instead of speaking, I ducked into the restroom and stayed there through much of the show. I didn't want anyone to know I was there with my family instead of a date, despite the fact that I wasn't yet allowed to date!

Thank you, Jesus, that most of the time Laurie appreciates the fact that her father and I aren't really humiliating. Some parents are. We know a mother who makes an obvious play for any boy her daughter dates. Another parent has been arrested repeatedly on gambling charges. Still another attended his son's homecoming football game drunk, and accompanied by a flashy girlfriend his son's age.

For teens who must deal with parents such as these, Lord, I ask your special blessings. Give them strength to cope. Let them realize that irresponsible parents don't reflect on one's own worth. Restore a sense of dignity, and of honor.

Help me to keep a sense of humor when Laurie finds me an embarrassment. Don't let me feel hurt or rejected; this, too, is a stage, and one that is almost over.

While it lasts, though, let me stand firm in reminding Laurie that I have rights, too: the right to wear that belt she thinks is dumb-looking; the right to sing old popular songs while I load the dishwasher; and the right to roller skate even if nobody else's mother does.

I even have the right to make mistakes—talking too loud in the shoe store, for one.

"Then, when that happens, we are able to hold our heads high no matter what happens and know that all is well, for we know how dearly God loves us, and we feel this warm love everywhere within us because God has given us the Holy Spirit to fill our hearts with his love" (Rom. 5:5).

Mom the Spy

Laurie was showing me a pair of silver pendant earrings. "Kerri got these for her mother's birthday," she explained. "I'm keeping them until Wednesday so they'll be a surprise."

"They're lovely," I commented. "But surely a box this small would be easy for Kerri to hide."

Laurie made a face. "She has absolutely no privacy! Her mother goes through her drawers, opens her mail, even listens in on some of her phone calls. She read Kerri's diary until Kerri found out and stopped keeping one." Laurie paused for breath. "I don't know what she thinks she'll find. Now Kerri keeps all her private stuff here, or at Beth's."

"Such as?"

"Oh, you know . . . " Laurie was purposely vague. "Letters, poems she's written, stuff like that."

It's hard for parents to realize that children have the same needs for privacy and space that we adults do. More, really, because secrets are part of being a teen. Muted phone calls to that special girlfriend, five-page letters from the boy met at camp, a daily journal of one's deepest thoughts and longings—all these are a normal phase in growing up.

In a way, though, I can understand why Kerri's mother feels she must snoop and pry. Teens can be so secretive! And I've read two articles by Christian counselors who actually suggest parents turn themselves into spies!

Lord, I'm sure there are valid reasons for invading a child's privacy: suspected drug use or shoplifting, perhaps. I even suppose there's an off-chance that Lance is hiding copies of an undesirable magazine under his mattress or that Laurie grows marijuana in her underwear drawer. But I have no reason to suspect either of them of such wrongdoing, so those are chances I'll have to take.

We've established mutual trust in our family, and I don't want to destroy it. I'm grateful for the large part of their lives that Lance and Laurie have chosen to share with me. I'll try to keep "hands off" the portion that is theirs alone.

Thank you, Lord, that private things are safe in our house.

"Treat others as you want them to treat you" (Luke 6:31).

Acting My Age

Mark's mother was at the program tonight. She's my age, but was apparently trying to look like Mark's sister. Bleached hair streamed over her shoulders; she wore a skimpy tube top and too-tight slacks; her eye makeup must have been applied with a trowel. The effect was ridiculous, and I know Mark saw some of the kids giggling and staring. I could read the humiliation in his eyes.

I wanted to take the woman aside and say, "Act your age!" Only, maybe, she didn't know how. I've felt that way a lot lately. I and everyone else knows I'm nearly forty—definitely middle-aged. And suddenly I'm not at all sure what "acting my age" really means.

Thanks to a fortunate combination of genes, my hair doesn't show much gray; when it does, I'll probably dye it, since my hair won't be the shimmery, lustrous gray some women have. My wash-and-wear curls are ageless, and I'd look silly in the long style Laurie begs me to try. But what about makeup? Should I use more now that I'm "mature"? Or less?

What about clothes? I've worn jeans and T-shirts for casual dress all my life. Must I give them up? If so, for what? I hate polyester pants! I've never worn a housedress, either, and I don't want to start now.

You see, Lord, I'm light years past "cute" (a term which never fit anyway), but I don't want to be dowdy, either. I don't want to be what Lance described as "one of those really old mothers—you know, fat, yellowish-gray hair, wearing one of those shapeless shirts."

Are there guidelines for growing old? A rule that says at twenty do this, at forty that, and at eighty something else?

Heavenly Father, don't let me sit in judgment (even in my mind!) on women who try too desperately to preserve the illusion of youth, or on those who go to the other extreme. Do guide my choice of clothes, hairstyles, and makeup so that I'm not an embarrassment to my family, friends, or to you.

Please, though, let me be myself! Let me remain free to dress in the way that suits the unique personality you have given me. And if it's okay, I'll keep my jeans.

"You are truly my disciples if you live as I tell you to, and you will know the truth, and the truth will set you free. . . . So if the Son sets you free, you will indeed be free" (John 8:31b, 32, 36).

Bags and Wrinkles

When Lance's high school graduation was only a few weeks away, it's approach made me acutely, painfully aware of my age. I was shocked to realize that I am what I considered *old* when I was Lance's age.

People refer to "growing old gracefully." I'm growing old (a glance in the mirror confirms that), but I'm not sure about the grace part. I do know that at this moment I don't like it. The aging process, with its ravages on youth and beauty, seems so unnecessary, so unfair. The inside me is still young and strong. Why can't my face and figure reflect that feeling?

I can't spend money on a facelift, but neither can I condemn the men and women who do. There are times when I truly hate the wrinkles around my eyes and the lines across my forehead. I watch my diet and I exercise regularly, but I am all too aware that nothing will restore the firm, attractive body of my youth.

Lord, forgive me, please, for being self-centered and vain; surely that's what this current preoccupation with looks is. I know that a Christian woman should be content with the real beauty that springs from a life lived in harmony with you. I know how I should be, and also that I'm not that way. I feel guilty about my attitude, and that guilt makes me feel unattractive inside as well as out.

It helps to think of women who are old but still vital and lovely. My mother is one. At seventy, she still swims, travels, and entertains. Thank you, too, for the examples of women in public life, women making valuable contributions to our world. They aren't young, because their jobs demand the experience and maturity that comes with age. And I've seen the faces of women whose lives have been totally devoted to your service. Their eyes hold a luminous beauty that is almost heavenly.

Help me to accept myself, Lord, sags and bags and wrinkles and all. Make me beautiful in ways that count, in loving, caring, serving, forgiving. Let my life radiate the joy I find in you.

Let me be old, even ancient. But please, not too soon. If you don't mind, could I discover the gray hairs and new wrinkles *gradually*? It will be easier that way.

"She is a woman of strength and dignity, and has no fear of old age" (Prov. 31:25).

Yesterday

I was cleaning a desk drawer when I found an old picture of Laurie and Beth. They had on Brownie uniforms and were totally absorbed in a game of "School." Laurie was reading *Tip and Mitten*, while Beth printed an "assignment" in her Big Chief tablet.

A hundred yesterdays flooded my mind! The games they played! "House," with Laurie's stuffed bears for children; "Restaurant," which depleted my silverware drawer; "Department Store," with my pearls draped on a doll mannequin. Sometimes they dressed Josie up in diapers and baby clothes and wheeled her around the yard. Other times they used their imaginations to combine book and television favorites, resulting in games such a "Pippi Longstocking visits the Little House on the Prairie."

The girls have been friends since they were three. When you saw one, you usually saw the other. Once they got identical outfits—green T-shirts trimmed in white, and striped slacks—hoping people would think they were twins. Despite the radical difference in hair and complexion, one woman actually did!

I remember the week they had mumps together. And the birthday when Beth's dad brought Laurie's gift in the back of a pickup—a huge box decorated like a circus wagon. Inside was the shaggy brown bear that still stands sentinal at the foot of Laurie's bed.

There was the time Beth cried so hard after school she couldn't tell me what was wrong. Laurie explained, "Eddie told her all Catholics were going to hell because they aren't really Christians. He said that since Beth is a Catholic, she and her whole family will burn in hellfire forever." I guess we talked about Jesus for an hour before Beth was reassured that God is interested in clean, committed hearts, not labels.

We had other theological talks, too. When Beth wondered if we would have clothes in heaven, Laurie informed her (disgustedly) that God would probably make all the girls wear dresses instead of jeans.

There were fights and tears, giggles and secrets—and there still are. Although both girls have branched out, making new friends and pursuing different activities, they are still each other's "best," and I hope they always will be.

Lord, it's different now, though. The little-girl days are gone forever. I never thought I'd miss them, but sometimes—such as today—I do.

"A true friend is always loyal, and a brother is born to help in time of need" (Prov. 17:17).

What Kind of World?

Today's newspaper carried a poignant letter from an elderly man to his teenage grandchildren. It began this way: "I want to apologize for the world I'm leaving you . . . for the mess my generation has created, but expects you to clean up." Among the problems he mentioned were: nations on the brink of nuclear war; a nearly bankrupt social security system; rapidly vanishing forest, wilderness, and agricultural lands; and social systems where human life and dignity are regarded as small things.

The message hit home. "What kind of world am I leaving Lance and Laurie?" I asked myself. "What should I have done to make the world they'll inherit a better one? Could I have helped them be better people, more competent to cope with the problems they will face?"

My answers made me ashamed. Politics leaves me bored. I vote, certainly, and support a few specific issues with letters and contributions. But my attitude toward government is usually, "Ho hum, who cares?" I've even neglected to do the thing God commanded: to pray regularly, fervently, and diligently for our leaders and those in authority.

I haven't been the best steward of the earth, either. Here in mid-America, where supplies of land, water, and fresh air seem inexhaustible, I've acted as if conservation wasn't my concern. I haven't even felt guilty about being part of a nation that outrageously overuses its share of the earth's resources. Far too often, my concern with the poor, hungry, and homeless of the world has begun and ended in my own little circle.

Now, as I'm brought face to face with the world that is my children's inheritance, I must also ask what kind of children I'm leaving the world. Will they be part of the solution? Or add to the problem?

A better world, I think, begins with strong families.

Have my husband and I provided a secure, loving home life to serve as a pattern for establishing future families? I wonder about my children's faith. Certainly they believe in Christ. But is their faith strong enough to help them meet the trials that are inevitable? Does their knowledge of Him make a real difference in their lives? I hope so, I pray so. But there are times when I'm not sure, when I believe I've failed miserably as a mother.

It isn't too late, is it? I can start to make the world—at least my part of it—a good one. I can increase my children's faith by example during those times when they won't listen to my words.

So let me be content to leave Lance and Laurie in your world, Lord, knowing that your love for all your creation is stronger than mine could ever be.

"Hear my prayer, O Lord; listen to my cry! Don't sit back, unmindful of my tears. For I am your guest. I am a traveler passing through the earth, as all my fathers were" (Ps. 39:12).

Conclusion

The End of the Beginning

Lance left for college last week. His car was piled high with clothes, towels, books, tapes and records, even food—all items essential for survival. He was smiling as he drove away, eager to start this brand new portion of his life.

Laurie started school today. She is looking forward to being an upperclassman. Her year promises to be as exciting as the others, and just as busy.

So I'm alone again. I dreaded this moment, but now that it's actually here it's not so bad.

Lord, you've been preparing me, haven't you? You've reminded me in a hundred ways that it is time to stand aside, to let Lance (and all too soon, Laurie) step out into the world.

You've pledged to take care of them for me—not only Lance and Laurie, but the others who are so familiar and dear: Beth, Kerri, Mark and Jason; and all the others who have been a part of their lives. Thank you for this assurance.

Thank you, too, for the year just past, for work and growth and pressure and laughter and tears, and even the times we screamed at each other. All these experiences add up to love.

This isn't the beginning of the end at all, is it? Rather, it is the end of the beginning. There's a new part of life ahead of me, too. Dear Lord, let it be a good part! Let me walk into it with confidence, with my eyes fixed firmly on you.